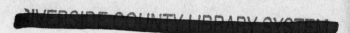

N

"James Baldwin had much to say. Sol Stein twice has made sure that he was heard."
—*The Washington Post*

"Legendary writer/editor/publisher Stein gives readers a backstage pass to the production of Baldwin's landmark essay collection *Notes of a Native Son*. [The book] will be extremely valuable to literary scholars."
—*Publishers Weekly*

"Baldwin's letters are extremely moving. . . . Stein's involving commentary is rich in fascinating literary history and sharp observations on racism, anti-Semitism, and their biracial friendship."
—*Booklist*

"Deliciously intimate . . . These letters, capturing the men at a pivotal moment in their careers and friendship, remind us that a cultural landmark like *Notes of a Native Son* is also the product of a fallible, questing human being who misspelled words and worried about his relatives just like the rest of us."
—*Kirkus Reviews*

"On behalf of the City of New York, I commend Sol Stein for providing readers with an opportunity to reflect on the legacy of the friendship and working rapport between two or our city's greatest authors. This tribute to the creative relationship between Stein and Baldwin celebrates the best of humanity, and illuminates the great productive potential of discourse between friends."
—Mayor Michael R. Bloomberg

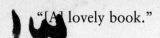

Native Sons

JAMES BALDWIN AND SOL STEIN

Native Sons

A Friendship That Created One of
the Great Works of the Twentieth Century:
Notes of a Native Son

One World
Ballantine Books • New York

2005 One World Books Trade Paperback Edition

Published in the United States by One World Books, an imprint of The Random
House Publishing Group, a division of Random House, Inc., New York.

ONE WORLD is a registered trademark and the One World colophon
is a trademark of Random House, Inc.

Originally published in hardcover in the United States by Ballantine Books, an imprint of
The Random House Publishing Group, a division of Random House, Inc., in 2004.

Grateful acknowledgment is made to Beacon Press and the William Morris Agency
for permission to reprint correspondence.

Library of Congress Cataloging-in-Publication Data

Baldwin, James, 1924–1987
Native sons : a friendship that created on of the great works of the twentieth century :
notes of a native son / by James Baldwin and Sol Stein.—1st ed.
p. cm.
ISBN 0-345-46936-4
1. Baldwin, James, 1924—Correspondence.   2. Baldwin, James, 1924—Friends
and associates.   3. Authors, American—20th century—Correspondence.   4. African
American authors—Correspondence.   5. Stein, Sol—Friends and associates.   6. Stein,
Sol—Correspondence.   7. Authorship—Collaboration.   I. Stein, Sol.   II. Title.

PS3552.A45Z485 2004
818'.5409—dc22   2003069091

Printed in the United States of America

www.oneworldbooks.net

2 4 6 8 9 7 5 3 1

Book design by Mercedes Everet

For my sons, Kevin, Jeff, Leland, Robin, David, and Andrew, and my daughter, Liz, who grew up understanding Jimmy Baldwin's last words in *Notes of a Native Son:* "This world is white no longer, and it will never be white again."

—S.S.

Our lives begin to end the day we become silent about things that matter.

—Martin Luther King Jr.

ACKNOWLEDGMENTS

This is a book by and about two friends, one of whom has allegedly been in Ferncliff Cemetery since 1987, but my conversations with him continued and were especially intense through the making of this book. When you read James Baldwin's letters, he will speak to you too.

I am grateful beyond easy measure to Gloria Baldwin Karefa-Smart, Baldwin's sister and executor, for her constant courtesy during the two years it took to prepare this book, and to Michael Schmidt Hayman for her daily assistance with the fragile originals. She brought order to the complex process of preparing this book for publication.

It is not easy to edit an editor who has been editing other people's books for half a century. Melody Guy's editorial notes were superbly brave, intelligent, and immediately helpful.

Sol Stein
Tarrytown, New York
September 18, 2003

CONTENTS

Native Sons

Notes of a Native American

The Story of a Friendship in Black and White

Sol Stein

> One thing you always have to keep in mind is how little you can take for granted. When one talks about the sixties, for example, one tends to assume that everyone knows what you're talking about, but, in fact, many of them were hardly born yet when the sixties were going on. That means you have to re-think everything as if it happened in ancient Rome or Greece.
>
> —James Baldwin in *Contact*,
> a publication of the University of Massachusetts
> at Amherst, January–February 1984

I am remembering five thousand people crowded into the Cathedral of St. John the Divine for James Baldwin's funeral, and I imagine my lifelong friend Jimmy and me watching that event, an elbow poking the other's rib for attention as in the old days when our lives intersected.

I knew James Baldwin first in our early teenage years, when I was thirteen and he was fifteen. It all began in the tower of De-Witt Clinton High School in the north Bronx at a time when students anywhere in the five boroughs of New York City didn't need to be bused anywhere but could elect to go to a high school of their choice. Baldwin, known then and since as Jimmy, went the distance by subway, bus, and foot from Harlem in Manhattan to DeWitt Clinton at the far northern edge of New York City, an exceptional school where his last formal education took place. In this day of failed busing, it is hard to imagine that in 1939 a poor boy could travel many miles to a different borough to seize an education he could not get locally.

When DeWitt Clinton first opened the doors at its present site in May of 1929, it claimed to be the largest secondary school for boys in the world. The three-story building and its athletic field and stadium occupied about twenty-six acres and had a single-session capacity of over five thousand students. A recently re-modeled room just off its library displays a picture gallery of onetime Clinton students that includes such luminaries as Paddy Chayevsky, Countee Cullen, Burt Lancaster, Ralph Lauren, Jan Peerce, Richard Rodgers, A. M. Rosenthal, Daniel Schorr, Neil Simon, and Lionel Trilling. Clinton was a garden in which black and white teenagers could become fast friends, an environment that a few years later made possible *Notes of a Native Son,* which in 1999 was selected by a distinguished panel as one of "the 100 best nonfiction books of the century."

Our home away from home was in what we called the Magpie Tower, the place where DeWitt Clinton's award-winning literary magazine, *The Magpie,* was edited by students as young as thirteen and fourteen. Our core group, besides Baldwin and me, included Richard Avedon and Emile Capouya, working under the tutelage of a faculty member, Wilmer Stone. Avedon was then a poet and shy. When we were called upon to sell the issue of January 1941, Avedon and I would stand in front of each classroom, Avedon silent, his hands clasped in front of him, while I recited a poem of his from memory. America had not yet formally entered World War II, but London was burning. Avedon's poem that lingers still in my memory is about the loss of a childhood friend in the firebombing of London. What we all wrote then is today mostly embarrassing, but the learning process was astonishing.

On Friday afternoons, after classes officially let out, the *Magpie* gang would assemble in the tower above the three floors of the school building to hear our faculty advisor read our stories aloud to us in the most boring monotone imaginable. We were eager to see our stories in print and were learning to take criticism in a most painful way that was also instructive, for we learned then what all writers must eventually learn, that the reader has to be moved by the words alone, without help from the histrionic talents of the author.

Stone's private critiques of our work could be withering. Avedon told me a couple of years ago that on one occasion Stone asked him what kind of reading matter his parents had lying around the house. Avedon mentioned magazines like *Good Housekeeping* and *McCall's.* Stone told him, "That's what's wrong with your writing." At that moment, Avedon said, he decided to give up writing and turned, brilliantly, to photography.

More than forty years later, in the preface to the 1984 edition of *Notes of a Native Son,* Baldwin begins, "It was Sol Stein, high school buddy, editor, novelist, playwright, who first suggested this book. My reaction was not enthusiastic: as I remember, I told him that I was too young to publish my memoirs. I had never thought of these essays as a possible book. . . . Sol's suggestion had the startling and unkind effect of causing me to realize that time had passed. It was as though he had dashed cold water in my face. Sol persisted, however. . . ."

I don't remember Baldwin's resistance to doing the book. I do remember the editorial process, helped by recently finding my line-by-line editorial notes and Baldwin's responses, which are included in the correspondence section of this book. Writers can be wary of editors they don't know well. By the time Baldwin and I had to deal with *Notes of a Native Son,* the overlay of a friendship of a dozen years made the process easier.

A friendship that endures might reasonably be defined as a

house in which disagreements are confined to an attic that can be opened for memoirs but never for continuation of a former argument. Baldwin and I came to our friendship with differences. He was black and I was white, he loved men and I loved women, he assumed his ancestors came to America in chains and I assumed my parents, who slipped over the border separately and illegally, came here because they had nowhere else to go. Despite the differences— we lived many miles apart—because of our friendship our families took a liking to each other. There are surviving photographs of Jimmy bouncing two of my pajama-clad children on his knee. I loved and admired Baldwin's mother, Berdis, and believed it was reciprocal even at our last warm meeting after Jimmy's death. Berdis visited with my family when Jimmy was abroad. I was welcome in Berdis's apartment on 131st Street in Harlem, but not by the policeman who stopped me outside and wanted to know what my white face was doing in that neighborhood.

Berdis had a secret that to my knowledge and Jimmy's say-so was never divulged: the identity of Jimmy's father. The now legendary stepfather Jimmy wrote about was the preacher who married Berdis, presumably legitimized her son, and gave her eight more children. My mother, Zelda Zam, enjoyed Jimmy's brightness, his dancing hands. Like Berdis Baldwin, she had her secret. According to family legend, in the old country, hiding in the cellar during a pogrom, through a crack in the door my mother saw her first fiancé killed by one of Petlyura's Cossacks. In America she had another secret I discovered as a child during the Great Depression. In the old country, my mother at a young age was the head of secondary evening schools in Kiev, the largest city in the Ukraine. To make a living in America she sold *Compton's Encyclopedia* door-to-door, and one day, when the Depression bottomed, I opened the heavy sample case she took to work every day and found the knee pads she wore when cleaning other people's floors. Baldwin's mother, Berdis, may also have done the same.

Jimmy Baldwin and I, both Depression-era kids, responded differently to food. At my mother's table, Jimmy would eat like a bird, one small piece at a time, taking two hours over a simple meal, while I devoured all of it in the first few minutes. One might suppose that Jimmy was stretching out the pleasure of food, while I was gulping it down before it vanished. One of my few memories of Depression eating was the time my mother and father planted the single orange my father had brought home on the table and said, "You eat. We'll watch."

Though both of my parents came from Russia, I had trouble identifying with my mother's motherland, just as Jimmy later had trouble identifying with Africa. I remember Baldwin's rising hope in *Nobody Knows My Name:* "Africa was now on the stage of history. This could not but have an extraordinary effect on [the morale of blacks], for it meant that they were not merely the descendants of slaves in a white, Protestant, and puritan country: they were also related to kings and princes in an ancestral homeland, far away." Africa let Baldwin down. The dark continent produced corrupt kings and corrupt princes who robbed their people and kept them poor. Tribalism unleashed the wholesale butchery of millions, while in America, which Baldwin acknowledged as his only homeland, a black American, Colin Powell, had ascended to a position of power a few hearts away from the presidency of his country, though inner cities remained inert cities, fatherless and poor. Everything changes slowly, and human nature not at all.

Growing up, I wanted so badly to be thought of as an American and not as a sometimes despised Jew. Baldwin could instantly be seen as black by anyone. To the onlooker, I had no visible marks that at once characterized me as Jewish. Blond from birth, soon enough I was six feet tall. Observers knew me to be Jewish only after they knew my name, which left time beforehand for strangers to make anti-Semitic remarks in my presence, assuming me to be one of them. It is quicker to be typed as black, as different, as not belonging. The sting of later recognition of a Jew who doesn't look particularly Jewish can be startling.

When I was seven, in the sweltering New York summer kids could get into the swimming pool of Evander Childs High School by lining up to pay four cents for admission. One day the older boy behind me on line had a metal Star of David attached to the handlebars of his bicycle. I asked him if he was Jewish. He reared back. He didn't know the insignia he had found and affixed to his bicycle was a Jewish star. He asked if I was Jewish. I nodded, at which point he raised his fist and exclaimed, "You killed Jesus Christ!" It was the first such exposure for me. I will mention one more. Early in my two years as a soldier during the last part of World War II and after, before going overseas I was stationed briefly at a post near the University of Illinois in Champaign. I no longer remember how I came to date the homecoming queen of the university, but we quickly became friends. During my time away from base, I read poetry to her. We saw each other several times before June Saylor, somewhat embarrassed, said her parents wanted to know where my parents came from. Full of youthful romance, dismayed and hurt, I fudged, but not enough to make me acceptable to June's parents, however acceptable I might have been to her. It occurred to me that if I'd been black, we'd never have dated, and the sting of ethnic rejection would not have belatedly smashed what may have been the beginning of a courtship.

For better, not for worse, Baldwin and I were here, native Americans, charged up, yearning to make it as Americans while trying to shake up America to make it a more congenial nest for the likes of us. Before each of us was a lover of specific people, we were lovers of language, which if delivered well can have even more immediate power than print. Franklin Roosevelt read Sam Rosenman's words with a mesmerizing authority that helped lift the sagging spirits of Americans in a bad time. Churchill's rhetoric, drafted by himself, defied Hitler and defeat. Martin Luther King Jr., in his preacher's delivery, announced his dream. Much has been made of Baldwin's having been a teenage preacher, an influence that is evident in his incantatory prose and his ability to address readers as if they were his congregation. Not enough has been made of his early mastery of the writer's main task, putting to paper what other people only think.

Laymen speak of a writer's style. Writers and editors speak of a writer's voice, a distinguishing way with words that is recognizable and consistent. As an editor, I was attracted to Baldwin's writing because of his voice and his writerly intelligence, his use of visual particularity to make us see the places and people he was writing about. Once his reader was lured into the experience, Baldwin would let loose insights that were startling in their candor. At the behest of the publisher, I wrote a prefatory note for *Notes of a Native Son,* in which I said, "In the jargon of writers, 'pieces' is the word used to describe articles, essays, and the uncategorizable writings that constitute the writer's baggage while he is traveling between major works. Yet of Lord Acton, for instance, such 'pieces' are all we have; fortunately, they inform each other as well as us and constitute a whole. That is also the virtue of James Baldwin's pieces, a frightening virtue in one so young." When I saw the prefatory note in galley proof, I ordered it removed on the grounds that Baldwin's work didn't need my introduction. One can't escape error that easily, for I recently found the *Library Journal* review of *Notes of a Native Son,* made from a bound galley of the book, and there was notice of the introduction that no longer existed in the book itself.

Toward the end of his life, Baldwin said *Notes of a Native Son* was of crucial importance in his struggle to define himself in relation to his society. "I was trying to decipher my own situation, to spring my trap, and it seemed to me the only way I could address it was not take the tone of the victim. As long as I saw myself as a victim, complaining about my wretched state as a black man in a white man's country, it was hopeless. Everybody knows who the victim is as long as he's howling. So I shifted the point of view to 'we.' Who is the 'we'? I'm talking about we, the American people."

In the world of publishing and bookselling, it was believed that books of essays did not sell. Part of the problem was that putting a binding around random essays made for a random reading experience. A book demanded cohesiveness. The reader had to feel he was on a discernible path from the first page to the last, which meant a lot of attention had to be paid to the order of the essays. In addition, the first and last essays had to be chosen carefully, for the mission of the first was to get the reader to read on, and the mission of the last was to leave the reader with a strong impression of the book.

If memory serves me, the autobiographical and justly famous first chapter of *Notes* had its origin in Knopf's publicity department asking Baldwin to fill in a lengthy questionnaire in connection with the publication of his first novel, *Go Tell It on the Mountain*. Baldwin was uncomfortable with any questionnaire, much less one about his life. He turned the questionnaire over onto its blank sides and in pen wrote, "I was born in Harlem thirty-one years ago. I began plotting novels at about the time I learned to read." That became the first essay in *Notes of a Native Son*.

For the last chapter we settled on "Stranger in the Village," which has lost none of its power in the half century since its publication. The village was in Switzerland, high up, detached from the world, "mountains towering on all four sides, ice and snow as far as the eye can reach. A white wilderness." The inhabitants had never seen a typewriter or a Negro. Everyone knew Baldwin came from America, but they didn't believe it because they'd long ago learned that black men came from Africa. Baldwin was seen as a living wonder and not as a human being. The children who shouted at him, "*Neger!*"—German for "black"—had no way of knowing how that word echoed. On a second visit, while some of the children made overtures of friendship, those who had been taught that the devil is a black man screamed in fear as Baldwin approached. In that essay Baldwin purposely creates unease in the reader, just as the experience he is relating created unease in him. In doing that Baldwin differentiated himself from writers who produce essays to get something off their chests. Baldwin, especially in his early work, concentrated on evoking emotion in the reader, the novelist's aim and the essayist's forte. Baldwin's imagination devises a mirror. When the Swiss villagers are astonished at his color, Baldwin thinks of white men arriving for the first time in an African village, and tries to imagine the astounded populace touching the white men's hair as the children in the Swiss village touched his. He imagines the Africans marveling at the color of the white man's skin as the Swiss villagers gape at his. It is Baldwin's ability to imagine such mirror images, his insight as a writer into the visions that people have of others and otherness, that enable readers who are not black to momentarily experience what a black man feels, and invites the black reader to grasp the origins of the white man's desperate clinging to a prejudice that drains both white and black of some of their humanity.

Baldwin was early on a master of resonance. The Swiss village becomes the West to which Baldwin feels so strangely grafted. He says the most illiterate among the villagers is related in a way that he is not to Dante, Shakespeare, Michelangelo, Aeschylus, Da Vinci, Rembrandt, and Racine. The resonance of that sentence charms the reader to gloss over its falsity. Baldwin in his first book was already part of what we now so reluctantly call Western culture. And many of the Swiss villagers would have had a hard time even identifying Dante or Aeschylus. Baldwin's theme then was the relatedness of the ingredients in the American bouillabaisse, how interdependent we are. My role as an editor was to help realize his intentions, and in the case of *Notes* to make certain that Baldwin's occasional essays for magazines were not abandoned to wastebaskets but preserved as a book, as it has been now for half a century.

Young and intolerant, I spoke against any essays that fell below a high standard. Baldwin wanted to include some pieces he had written for *The New Leader* that did not meet that standard. I was fighting on two fronts at the time because I was also editing Leslie Fiedler's first book of essays, *An End to Innocence,* and applied the same standards to Fiedler's very different voice.

Friendly arguments with Baldwin ensued mainly when he was traveling somewhere in the world and I was trying to calm the publisher's demand for his money back because Baldwin was so late delivering expected material. Lateness was a conspicuous feature in Baldwin's life, and one had to get used to it. Finally, the book was ready, and I arranged to get reviews from *Time* and *Newsweek*. The Associated Press chose *Notes* as its Book of the Week, and I was eager to get this news to Baldwin. I ended one letter—probably sent to him in care of American Express somewhere—"I tried to pray for you, but God said he didn't know where to find you." I added a P.S. saying my wife sends her love "because women are always forgiving."

Notes of a Native Son was published in 1955, seven years before I was to have my own imprint of Stein and Day. Publication of *Notes* came about as a result of the publishing evolution that brought trade paperbacks into prominence. The publisher of *Notes* was the Beacon Press in Boston, with which I had a strange contract. It designated me pretentiously as the "Originator and General Editor of Beacon Paperbacks." The Director of the Press at the time was one of the remarkable publishers of the century, Melvin Arnold, who later became the president of Harper & Row. The license I received from Melvin Arnold to publish writing I admired in a new format, the book-size paperback, was a significant advantage to a new essayist like Baldwin. With *Notes of a Native Son* the young James Baldwin stepped into distinguished company on a small list that included André Malraux, Eric Bentley, Leslie Fiedler, Sidney Hook, George Orwell, Arthur Koestler, Simone Weil, and Bertram D. Wolfe, which likely reinforced Baldwin's debut as an essayist.

It is commonly agreed that Baldwin's essays were more successful in their achievement than his fiction, and his first book of essays is certainly the most honored of his accomplishments. His fiction never again attained the level of his first novel, *Go Tell It on the Mountain.* In both his fiction and nonfiction, as time went on Baldwin allowed the preacher in him to overtake the writer. His most popular work at the time of its publication, *The Fire Next Time,* allowed the intrusion of hyperbole: "blacks simply don't wish to be beaten over the head by the whites every instant of our brief passage on this planet." I heard this as the language of soapbox speech, and thought, *Give me back Baldwin the writer.*

Baldwin eventually came to a similar conclusion. In 1970, in an interview with Ida Lewis, editor in chief of *Essence* magazine, she said, "You became the famous James Baldwin, writer and black spokesman." To which Baldwin replied, "Yes, I played two roles. I never wanted to be a spokesman, but I suppose it's something that had to happen. But that is over now." Lewis prodded him to be more specific. He replied, "Because of what I had become in the minds of the people, I ceased to belong to me. Once you are in the public limelight . . . you have to realize you've been paid for . . . to save myself I finally had to leave [America] for good."

Among the black American writers who had fled to Paris, he was the only one who had an important influence on the civil rights movement back home. He organized a protest march of black expatriates—writers, artists, musicians—to the American embassy. And finally he felt he had to return home to participate in the historic March on Washington. Baldwin had learned to be an effective public speaker, using as few carefully chosen words as he could, speaking them slowly, using silences to build tension. He played with the audience's emotions, drawing loud approval from strangers. Such resonance warms both the audience and the speaker but does not measure up to the excitement of fashioning thought into words with precision. Writing was Baldwin's mission and his joy. As a public speaker, he began to see what might be behind the scrim of his fear. His friend Malcolm X was killed, Martin Luther King Jr. was killed, his friend Medgar Evers was killed, John and Bobby Kennedy were killed, and Baldwin the public man was justly frightened to continue on public platforms. What he wanted most was seclusion with his typewriter, to be what he had wanted to be from the beginning, not a speech-maker but an honest man and a good writer.

The fact that Baldwin's writings during his public career lack some of the power of his earliest work does not diminish his accomplishment. Neither Hemingway nor Fitzgerald got better with every book. *Notes of a Native Son* has not dated the way so many books of its period have. Its insights are relevant today when separatism sometimes threatens the image of America as harbor and sanctuary. Baldwin the ex-preacher taught best when he preached least.

Peterborough, New Hampshire, is the site of the MacDowell Colony, an oasis for creative people established by the widow of the composer Edward MacDowell early in the twentieth century. The Colony provides composers, painters, and writers with an opportunity to work in quiet comfort, away from the workaday world. In 1952 I'd had a playwriting fellowship at MacDowell to complete my first play. Arriving there, I was in for a surprise.

There was one other playwright at MacDowell, Thornton Wilder, whose *Our Town* was then being shown somewhere in the world every day of every year. Wilder became the newcomer's mentor. He helped me to understand how a writer does research as a Peeping Tom. He took me to a country square dance in New Hampshire, where family members danced with each other. From an empty balcony, Wilder pointed out the sexual nuances within the families, the mother with the son, the father with the daughter, as they danced the evening away. Wilder said good plays entertain, bad ones instruct. He insisted that I see as many bad plays as I could. The New Dramatists organization provided that opportunity, enabling me to see some sixty plays free of charge in a two-year span. Wilder's lengthy handwritten notes on my play survived, as did the play, a verse drama that was staged the following year at the ANTA Theater in New York with a brilliant cast and won the Dramatists Alliance prize for "the best full-length play of 1953." It was also performed in California, where it received seven out of seven favorable reviews. To my later regret I wasn't there to see it because I was tied to a daytime job, and with three young children I could not afford the big dent in my paycheck a trip to California would involve. It did, however, catch the attention of the Theater Guild, which later redounded to the advantage of Baldwin and me.

I recommended the MacDowell Colony to Baldwin as a good place to work, though I couldn't guarantee Thornton Wilder would be there to mentor him. In 1954, Baldwin and I managed to be at MacDowell at the same time. There is a photograph of the assembled MacDowell artists that includes a youthful Baldwin and Stein taken the year that *Notes of a Native Son* was put together. One day, on separate missions, Baldwin and I headed into New York City, then a six-hour drive away. Halfway there we drove into a biblical-size deluge. The roads quickly flooded, and electric cables came crashing down onto the flooding roads.

State troopers warned us it was dangerous to get out of the car. Baldwin and I talked about turning back, but the road back appeared as treacherous as the road forward, so forward we went. In minutes, we were up and over the crest of a hill. Beneath us the road had disappeared into a river overflowing its banks. As we rolled downhill toward the river with minimal traction, Baldwin sang out a lament, "This is going to be a sad day for American literature."

Seconds later we could discern two neatly parallel lines in the roiling water below us. I couldn't stop the car. We guessed what we were seeing had to be the cables that supported the narrow and invisible bridge, and so I steered as best I could to enter the water between those two lines. It was a good guess. The car was partly submerged but moving, and eventually we were across and onto land. We found the road, avoided the downed wires, and kept driving, with more than a dozen books each still to be written.

Just a few years later, the play that I wrote at MacDowell, *Napoleon,* proved to be useful to Baldwin and me. In 1957 Baldwin and I, non-collaborators by temperament, wrote a television play together, *Equal in Paris,* which is being published in this book for the first time nearly half a century after it was written. How was it that two such independent strivers wrote a play together? Of course, we'd been good friends for more than fifteen years and, more important, had the experience of working together as author and editor of *Notes of a Native Son.* What each of us brought to the collaboration table was different. Though the underlying story was Baldwin's, written as a nonfiction essay in *Notes,* I'd had the greater experience in writing for the theater and television.

The Theater Guild, then a force in the American theater, with an admiring report of my *Napoleon* in its files, assigned me to write a dramatization of a novel for the Guild's television showcase, the *U.S. Steel Hour.* They then commissioned me to write what became, under distinguished but other auspices, a Broadway play entitled *A Shadow of My Enemy,* which proved to be more than a bit ahead of its time. While this controversial play drew favorable reactions from the likes of Eric Bentley and Richard Rovere, it also drew pickets, which is not exactly an inducement to casual theatergoers. At the National Theater in Washington, opening night drew four justices of the Supreme Court, apparently an unprecedented event. Henry Fonda, who was starring in a two-person play called *Two for the Seesaw* at the Shubert Theater in Washington, used to visit our stars' dressing rooms and declare with certainty that we would be a success in New York and *Seesaw* would be a failure. His play ran for two years in New York, ours for a single week. On closing night, after the show I saw Roger Stevens, the lead producer, stride across the lobby straight at me. Considering the amount of money he must have lost on the play, I was ready to defend myself. Instead, Stevens, ever the gentleman, said, "Write another like this and I'll produce it."

Baldwin and I wrote the play *Equal in Paris* because we had reason to believe that it might be produced by the Theater Guild. The protagonist of our play was a black man of twenty-five we called Billy Ade, to whom we would lend Baldwin's experience in Paris as in his essay of the same name. In that essay, Baldwin never alluded to his homosexuality. To meet what we thought of as the requirements of a story acceptable to television, we introduced a sentimental heterosexual love interest for the protagonist. Nevertheless, the heart of the play deals with what was perhaps the central issue of Baldwin's early experience as a tormented young man who wanted to be seen as an American and not as a Negro. Seething with rage at the way he and other blacks were beheld and treated in the States, and fearful of his sometimes violent reactions to prejudice, Baldwin had fled to France, where Richard Wright had gone before him and where, it was said, blacks were perceived differently. In Paris, for a period of eight days Baldwin was treated like a white Frenchman. He was accused of receiving a stolen bedsheet from a young white bohemian we named Square in the play. Both of them were arrested. Baldwin thought the arrest was a mistake, that they would momentarily be released from the tiny cell in which it was almost impossible to sit or lie down. They were held incommunicado. Baldwin was not allowed to phone the American embassy or a lawyer he'd met. Later, handcuffed, Baldwin was transferred to an enclosed shed in which the human detritus of the Paris streets was detained, and in the center of which was a great hole that was the common toilet. Finally, he was taken to a prison twelve kilometers outside of Paris, where, absent a tradition of habeus corpus, he was still kept from contacting a lawyer to get him out. Finally, through a prisoner being let go, he was able to get word out to the lawyer he'd met. Released after eight days that included Christmas, Baldwin decided to head home to America, where, bad as it was for blacks at the time, its laws at least provided civil rights that were absent in France. Baldwin recorded that experience in his essay "Equal in Paris," which we included in *Notes of a Native Son*.

Our collaboration was probably enabled at least in part by our common interest in playwriting. We both received help from the then little-known New Dramatists Committee, which arranged for playwrights to see their work in progress performed by professional actors. We both benefited from parallel experiences with Elia Kazan when we were appointed production observers on plays Kazan was directing. Baldwin was to witness every stage of the production of Archibald MacLeish's *J.B.* and I every rehearsal of Tennessee Williams's *Cat on a Hot Tin Roof*.

The managing director of the Theater Guild at the time was William Fitelson, a feisty Napoleon of the theater, a prominent show business lawyer who devoted time and money to civil rights causes. He had not yet met Baldwin. Fitelson exerted his power in New York theatrical circles in eccentric ways. Once when my wife and I were the sole dinner guests at his Greenwich Village house, he asked if we'd care to hear some music. I expected him to turn on his hi-fi set. Instead, Fitelson went sprightly to his phone. Shortly, Burl Ives showed up at the door, guitar in hand, to sing for our small gathering. Fitelson was also known for summoning various New York intellectuals to be his guests at a Broadway show on a few hours' notice and expecting them obediently to show up, which they did both for the free tickets and so as not to displease Fitelson, who seemed to take pleasure in an entourage to whom he could serve theatrical summonses. I wondered how he might react to Baldwin, to whom appointments were indistinct invitations, and who almost always showed up late.

Fitelson was also known for having his assistant, Anna May Franklin, accompany him, pad in hand, on the five- or six-block walk along Fifth Avenue from his law offices to the Theater Guild's offices on Fifty-third Street. As he dictated letters and memoranda, his loyal assistant tried to keep pace and scribble shorthand at the same time without bumping into people. Fitelson was a quirky mixture of compassion and arrogance. He gave money and time generously to oddball charities neglected by the mainstream. He had difficult relations with his children but took other people's children under his wing. One noon hour, he dropped into my office without advance warning and found me in a state. I don't recall what had thrown me into a funk, but Fitelson immediately phoned his secretary to cancel his appointments for the balance of the afternoon and took me to his club, where he submitted me to the steam room, the pool, and food, leaving me grateful for his grace and allowing me to reenter the world in a better state. Sometime later, the Theater Guild commissioned me to dramatize a novel for its *U.S. Steel Hour.* Meanwhile, Baldwin had had a play of his, *The Amen Corner,* produced at Howard University. Unbeknownst to Baldwin or me, these were all steps toward our collaboration on the play script, the only collaboration the high school buddies ever undertook except for Baldwin's collaboration with Richard Avedon in 1964 for a book entitled *Nothing Personal,* in which Baldwin's strong text and Avedon's equally strong pictures seem to have nothing to do with each other.

The first thing Baldwin and I wrote was a twenty-seven-page story we called "Dark Runner" that reads like a story because neither Baldwin nor I had a proclivity toward the kind of bare-bones synopsizing common in the film and television industries. With encouragement from Fitelson, we then wrote the play and called it by the same name as the essay it was derived from, "Equal in Paris." Having read the script, Fitelson summoned Baldwin and me to a lunch meeting to discuss the project. It seemed as if we had a clear chance of the final script being produced by the Theater Guild. Then Fitelson's assistant dropped the first bomb: None of the restaurants Fitelson frequented in Manhattan would allow a black man in.

When a restaurant was finally found that would seat the three of us, Fitelson announced his good news. He was prepared to go forward with the television play we'd written—with one proviso. The central character, that young black we'd named Billy Ade, had to be changed to white.

This, of course, made no sense. Changing the black man to white would undermine the main point of *Equal in Paris,* in which the young black protagonist is treated like any white Frenchman. We shelved the project in disgust.

I have reservations about the play, as any writer would about work done half a century earlier. If my friend Baldwin were still alive and we worked on updating the script, the protagonist's gayness would not be fudged. Nor would there be some of the sentimentality that was superimposed on the story. Writing is rewriting, and with the luxury of time, habitual rewriters like Baldwin and myself would have our work cut out, improving the script with the craft we'd gathered in a lifetime of writing.

In the original essay, there is no indication that Baldwin was gay. Early in his life he did have relations with both men and women. Perhaps I intuited his gayness from his extravagant and elegant arm movements until one day he declared, "I've got three strikes against me, I'm black, ugly, and gay."

Four decades after the script was written, while preparing my archives for Columbia University, I came across the original of the story we called "Dark Runner," and finally the script of the play *Equal in Paris.* The grafted love story and the sentimental ending could today be dealt with swiftly if Baldwin were alive and the old friends could collaborate for a few hours more. Like the essay it is based on, the play reflects in dramatic form Baldwin's view that first brought him to public attention. The story and the play included in this volume have not been tampered with, because they dramatize an experience Baldwin had early in his life that may explain why, despite the hard road that race relations has traveled in America, the result of that evolution still sets an example for places in the world where relations between races remain primitive and deadly.

Baldwin and I continued to share an interest in the theater, which never shared quite the same interest in us, though we both had plays produced on Broadway and elsewhere. Our friendship survived. The Theater Guild did not.

In 1960, I was editor of *The Mid-Century,* a magazine sponsored by an upper-brow book club that no longer exists. The magazine's principal writers were W. H. Auden, Jacques Barzun, and Lionel Trilling. I edited their reviews of books, and they edited mine. When Baldwin's second book of essays, *Nobody Knows My Name,* was about to be published by the Dial Press, with some trepidation I volunteered to review it. Friends should not review each other's books but do. This review had an astonishing consequence. I wrote it under the title "I Know Your Name." When it was in proof in June of 1961, I took it to Washington, D.C., where Baldwin was addressing a Freedom Riders rally in a church. Baldwin and I had agreed to meet for dinner afterward. After his speech, for the next two hours Baldwin autographed napkins and odd bits of paper for mothers carrying sleeping babies in their arms. I began to realize what it meant to be a public person, a balm for the ego and a drain on life's time. At our belated dinner, I showed Baldwin the galley with my review of *Nobody Knows My Name* with the stipulation that if it displeased him in any way I would cancel the review. We disagreed heartily about one passage in particular, I now forget which, but Baldwin, smiling, said, "Print it. I'll answer you." His next book was *The Fire Next Time,* first published in *The New Yorker.* My copy of *Nobody Knows My Name* is inscribed "For Sol:—In honor of the splendidly disputed passage. Love, Jimmy." Then he added, "God help us." Our friendship never wavered despite our disagreements, nor did it elicit retribution when, unbeknownst to me, Baldwin undertook to comment on a novel of mine, *The Childkeeper,* in his book *The Devil Finds Work.*

When Baldwin returned to the States from a period abroad he would drop by whatever office I was working in. In late 1961, Baldwin came by *Mid-Century*'s offices at a critical time in my life there. The absentee owner of The Mid-Century Book Society, Arnold Bernhard, funded the company to enjoy the companionship of cultured men such as Barzun, Trilling, and Auden. His cultural contacts established, Bernhard couldn't fathom why he had allowed himself to give away 49 percent of the company to the book club's editors and to me, and proposed a few changes that would leave him with 90 percent of the company instead of 51 percent. The only barrier he encountered was me, who had been reading a book called *Expulsion or Oppression of Business Associates: "Squeeze-Outs" in Small Enterprises.* Trying to find an excuse for firing me, Bernhard moved a staff accountant into my office to be within earshot of any conversations I might have. My first visitor under these new circumstances was my old friend James Baldwin. After we greeted each other, Baldwin said loud enough for the accountant to hear, "Who is that mother and what the fuck is he doing eavesdropping on us?"

The expression on the accountant's face at that moment was gratifying. Shortly after Baldwin's visit, a lawyer named Bertram Mayers sued Bernhard on my behalf, and quickly won a settlement that happily became the seed money for founding the publishing firm of Stein and Day, which I superintended for more than a quarter of a century. The young accountant—I can still hear Baldwin laughing at the snooper—took over running Mid-Century, grew a beard as a cultural appendage that might please the ladies, added newly tolerated sex books to the cultural mix, had *The Mid-Century* magazine's elegant appearance redesigned into a commercial format, and in short order brought the company to its knees.

It cannot have escaped notice that the title of this essay is "Notes of a Native American." I am advised by good authority that the largest population of American Indians is in the Los Angeles area, and they refer to themselves as Indians, not Native Americans, which is properly a description of everyone born here. I am a native American by virtue of having been born in Chicago, Illinois, and my friend Baldwin was a native American by virtue of having been born in New York. I don't refer to the Italians I grew up among as Italian-American, or my Irish friends as Irish-American, nor do I like to be designated a Jewish-American, which is most often used by people who don't like Jews. By the same reasoning, I am uncomfortable trying to think of Baldwin as an African-American. Both at the outset of his writing career and toward the end, he emphasized the fact that when he referred to "we" he meant Americans. That should not be as surprising as it seems to some. The overriding theme of the United States until the second half of the twentieth century was *E pluribus unum,* out of many one. The country was proud to be a melting pot of ethnicities. We were glad to witness the slow erosion of the ethnic prejudices that were part of the baggage brought to our shores by the waves of immigrants, who found some doors shut by the original European settlers who wanted freedom, as it turned out, mainly for themselves.

The last great public event in Baldwin's life that I was witness to was his sixtieth-birthday celebration at the University of Massachusetts at Amherst. I had a hugging reunion with his mother, Berdis, and his brother David, who'd become a friend three decades earlier, and with Jimmy, who introduced me around as his "high-school buddy." I was saddened that among the celebrants there were too few white faces, for I'd thought that by that time a celebration of Baldwin's contribution to American letters would not be so segregated. At the dinner that evening, at one point the master of ceremonies announced the presence of several people seated at the tables. When he came to Sol Stein, identified as the editor and publisher of *Notes of a Native Son,* Maya Angelou, seated at a table front and center, stood up, turned in my direction, and started applauding, and soon the entire assembly joined in the applause, a reward far greater than any other in my memory since the years-long struggle to bring *Notes* to publication.

In the Cathedral of St. John the Divine, the place of my formal good-bye to my friend of a lifetime, my wife and I were asked by David Baldwin, Jimmy's closest brother, to sit with the family, which we did until an usher came over and asked us to move to a different section, facing the rear of the cathedral, not quite the back of the bus. We were seated next to a white woman Baldwin had known in Paris. People who watched the funeral on television said our white faces were conspicuous in a sea of black. Our presence had somehow survived, and if Jimmy had been there to witness it, he would have laughed.

The Correspondence

Mainly Concerning the Editing and Publication of
Notes of a Native Son

Headnotes by Sol Stein

At the time that I edited and arranged for the publication of Baldwin's *Notes of a Native Son,* I was not employed by any publishing house, nor had I ever been. In my innocence, when I read something that pleased me greatly, my impulse was to share it. Word of mouth to friends wasn't enough. I needed the means to reach readers I didn't know. And so in 1953 I flew without license into an occupation I knew little about. Without experience to steer me, I was open to an amateur's innovation.

Paperbacks in the 1940s and early 1950s were rack-size pocket books sold mainly on newsstands and in drugstores. Transient entertainments far outnumbered books of lasting interest. However, in the '50s, a glimmer of hope for what I thought of as my kind of book shone in the halls of a commercial publishing house. Two editors with brows above the common level, Jason Epstein, then at Doubleday, and Nathan Glazer, later a distinguished professor at Harvard, were planning a series of pocket-sized books of quality that would sell mainly in bookstores.

I arranged a meeting with Glazer, whom I knew, and told him

Part of this introduction is adapted from "The Responsibilities of the Publisher" in my book *How to Grow a Novel,* St. Martin's Press, 1999.

of some of the books I would like to see in what became Anchor Books. I led with a proposal to rescue a near corpse, Bertram D. Wolfe's *Three Who Made a Revolution,* which had been published unsuccessfully some years earlier by the Dial Press, sold about a thousand copies, and for all practical purposes died. I was anxious to see his remarkable book back in print because of my belief that if a work is good enough, failure to sell the first time around should energize the author or publisher to try a different route. Glazer said they couldn't do the Wolfe book in Anchor because it was so long it would have to appear in three pocket-size volumes, and they'd have to sell more than thirty-five thousand copies of each to break even. I was heartsick. Should an important book be entombed because of its length?

Within days I came up with a plan to republish serious books by photo-offsetting them from the original editions in roughly the same size as the original books, saving typesetting costs, and using paperback covers. This could change the economic feasibility of republishing good books. They could now be profitable at runs under ten thousand copies, which made it feasible to take a chance on a far larger number of deserving books. It occurred to me that worthy unpublished work might also benefit from that new format because with the hardcover and large-format paperback being approximately the same size, they could be published in hardcover and large-format paperback simultaneously, with the thought that the hardcover would produce reviews and library sales, and the paperback would appeal to students and others for whom paper covers were then the format of choice because of price and because many young people of that generation didn't want to accumulate property (when people were on the move, paperbacks could be left behind).

By chance, as executive director of the American Committee for Cultural Freedom, I had supervised the writing of a topical book by two writers of different political affiliations. The book,

McCarthy and the Communists, by James Rorty and Moshe Decter, was published by the Beacon Press of Boston and had a run of thirteen weeks on *The New York Times* best-seller list. Beacon seemed a good place to try out my new idea.

I phoned Melvin Arnold, the director of the Beacon Press, an intellectual with a taste for controversy and experiment. In those days I kept an egg timer on my desk to monitor the length of my long-distance calls. Within three minutes, Mel Arnold said he'd fly down to New York to discuss my plan. Soon after, I was given a contract as "originator and general editor" of a new series of what were then called library-size paperbacks, a quaint name that didn't last long, and which, like their smaller cousins of quality, soon became known as trade paperbacks.

Within months, I faced my first audience of salesmen with my initial list of four books. I showed the covers. The salesmen laughed. They pooh-poohed the whole idea. They said the book-size paperbacks looked like European books, not American books; paperbacks were pocket books, and how the hell did you get those larger paperbacks into a pocket? And since one of the books, Wolfe's *Three Who Made a Revolution,* had sold only a thousand copies in hardcover, clearly a failure, what was the point of doing it in paperback? That was the book of eight hundred pages that my friend at Anchor Books had said was not economically feasible. Plus it contained photographs. The price would have to be $2.95. Who ever heard of charging $2.95 for a paperback? (In 1999 the same book in paperback was $14.95.) At the top of the front cover, I had put a quote by Edmund Wilson, then the leading literary critic of the United States, who called *Three Who Made a Revolution* "the best book in its field in any language." I chose that quote because Edmund Wilson had written a book on that same subject, and he was, in effect, saying that Wolfe's book was better than his own.

The sales force was still not convinced. As I described the

books onstage in front of the sales force, I waited for someone in the wings to use a hook to yank me off the platform like a vaudeville performer whose act had flopped. To his everlasting credit, Melvin Arnold gave me the green light for the series despite this cold reception from his salesmen. The first four books appeared in 1955. In the new format, Bertram Wolfe's book sold half a million copies in five years, and was adopted in Russian-studies courses in most American colleges and universities. Two of the early books were books of essays. The first was Leslie Fiedler's *An End to Innocence* and the other James Baldwin's *Notes of a Native Son*. Both books established their authors' reputations and are still available to readers half a century later.

As a result of the success of the new kind of paperback at the Beacon Press, Melvin Arnold was invited to do the same for the firm then known as Harper & Row (today HarperCollins). He eventually became its president before he retired to a forest in Oregon, where, when last seen there by me, in his eighties, he was still lifting weights and the spirits of others. He used to send me one copy each of the new trade paperbacks, the offspring of my offspring, addressed "To Grandfather," until my shelves begged off because their burden was too great.

The letters that follow provide the reader with a back-stage view of the process that introduced *Notes of a Native Son* to its place in the world. Baldwin's substantive letters begin on page 53.

May 23, 1955

During most of the correspondence between the Beacon Press in Boston and me when I was serving as editor of *Notes of a Native Son,* I was in New York and communicated with Melvin Arnold and others at the press by mail. When my presence was needed—for instance, at sales meetings—I would fly up for the day. To give the twenty-first-century reader a sense of that period, imagine this. I'd drive to LaGuardia Airport, park my car on a strip of grass, and walk less than a hundred yards to the plane headed for Boston. The trip took thirty-two minutes in the air. On return, I'd walk over to my car and drive off.

Prices were a bit different, too.

In the letter, Felix refers to Felix Morrow, Beacon's lead salesman. Ed Darling was Beacon's sales manager, but no one really managed Felix Morrow, who knew it all.

May 23, 1955

Dear Mel,

Add another top seller to your September list:

NOTES OF A NATIVE SON by James Baldwin

Everybody loves the title. Suggest for cover full page blow-up photo
of Baldwin. Shall I get one and airmail directly to cover artist, or
what? Best photo of Baldwin is one that appears on both paperback and
hard cover version of GO TELL IT ON THE MOUNTAIN (Knopf - New Amer. "ibrary).
Have to work fast, Baldwin only in town few days. Essays look terrific.
"Notes of a Native Son" will be the concluding chapter...never before published.
Checked Felix on idea of jacketxkdxx....says it's terrific from his sales
point of view: the Negro face and the title superimposed.

Am assembling blurbs on Baldwin for Ed Darling.

Would you want to hold back paper version 6 months if Readers Subscription
requires it? Or would you prefer simultaneous issue. On this one, suggest
we get early galleys to Book-of-the-Month Club also. E ought to think in
terms of a blow-up poster (face and title) for display in Negro college bookstores,
etc.

Please forgive telegraphese. Hurrying to make last mail.

Best,

May 26, 1955

This letter refers to eight essays. The final book contained
eleven essays. It was a bit nervy for the neophyte editor to jump
into the publisher's end of the business, for instance, appearance and pricing. The hardback of *Notes of a Native Son* was
priced at $2.75. The paperback, published later, was $1.25.

William Phillips was one of the founding editors of *Partisan Review,* probably the leading intellectual journal of its generation.

May 26, 1955

Mr. Melvin Arnold
The Beacon Press
Boston 8, Massachusetts

Dear Mel:

Haven't been able to reach you by phone today. Finished working over Jim Baldwin's NOTES OF A NATIVE SON late last night. Today and tomorrow Baldwin is working on certain minor revisions which we agreed on. I am happy to say that he was extraordinarily pleased with the arrangement of the pieces that I suggested. He was able to dig up for me a large photograph—an incredibly good one and better than the one Knopf used. Everyone who has seen it agrees that it would make a perfect jacket, better than the Schweitzer one, because with the title it tells the story. It would be hard for someone who sees this not to pick up the book and thumb through a few pages. This would be such a powerful jacket that I think we ought to do our utmost to have it made up before the sales conference. I'm still waiting for word on this from you.

Baldwin has one of the toughest agents in town, Helen Strauss of the William Morris Agency. I will have a lot of back and forth with her on the contracts. I'd suggest that these be prepared as quickly as possible, both for the hard and soft-covered editions. The book itself will be shorter than Fiedler's—eight essays instead of thirteen. But Baldwin and I agree that it would be a mistake to add another essay—one that does not fit what is now a clear cut conceptual arrangement. On the hard-covered edition, I would suggest that we use a larger typeface than the Fiedler book and spread out the words a bit!! Perhaps we also ought to use a heavier stock paper. The Baldwin book ought probably to sell for $2.75 and possibly 95¢ in paper, if it can be managed from the production end.

This is a suggestion for another new book to be entitled LITERATURE AND SOCIETY, to be edited with a special introduction by William Phillips and will be a compila-

tion of pieces about Joyce, Proust, Tolstoy, Dostoevsky,
etc. from PR and express its position: a social view of
literature. As background for your consideration of this
proposal, you should know that the first PR Reader had
several printings and sold 8000 copies in hard covers, of
which 1000 were sold by PR itself as part of a subscription program campaign. PR has also published three pam-
phlets which sold at $1 each and the sales have averaged
6000 for each pamphlet. Phillips is of the opinion that
this book would be consciously seeking out a good college
market for an auxiliary text on the best criticism available of the social implications of the greatest modern
writers. How do you feel about this for the Arts, Letters, and Society series?

                    Best,

                    Sol Stein

SS:bm

July 26, 1955

In the following letter, I am still trying to get the missing chapter for *Notes of a Native Son* from Baldwin. In the meantime I am suggesting a new Baldwin essay to be published in my Mid-Century series of one-dollar hardcover essays by well-known authors.

MacDowell Colony
Peterborough, N. H.
July 26, 1955

Miss Jane Wilson
William Morris Agency
1740 Broadway
New York 19, N. Y.

Dear Miss Wilson: re James Baldwin - NOTES OF A NATIVE SON

This will acknowledge receipt of your letter of July 21, 1955
and the check for $300 representing the return of money advanced by
me to Mr. Baldwin.

For several days now I've been trying to reach Mr. Baldwin
at the New Dunbar Hotel in Washington without success. The Beacon
Press is understandably anxious about the last chapter of the
manuscript, promised more than a month ago, particularly in view
of the scheduled publication date of October 26.

Miss Strauss may also want to know that I am prepared to
give Mr. Baldwin $500 for a single article-length essay to be
called "Letter to my Younger Brother," which I have discussed
in the past with Mr. Baldwin and which he seemed interested in
doing. This would be included in a series of "Mid-Century Essays"
which I am editing; the first contributor is Lionel Trilling.

If Mr. Baldwin would find it more convenient to work in the
Colony here or in Peterborough (he worked here last summer and
produced his play in record time), I think that could be arranged
and I believe the Beacon Press would be willing to pay for his
fare if it meant getting the rest of the manuscript pretty soon.

                    With all best wishes ,

                              Sincerely,

                              Sol Stein

August 1, 1955

The following pages are my editorial notes for the essay that
became "Autobiographical Notes," the first chapter of *Notes*.
Had I been an experienced editor or diplomat at the time, I
would have made these as *suggestions* instead of announcing
the changes as faits accomplis subject to reinstatement if Baldwin disagreed.

Of the suggestions, Baldwin accepted twenty and let three
stand as is. As writer and editor, I've been on both sides of the
editorial exchange. Once a powerful editor had eleven sections
of a novel of mine set in italics even though italics in more than
short bursts become difficult to read. I had to call on my onetime friendship with the head of that large publishing firm to
get the type restored to normal. Baldwin and I, however,
seemed to weather our editorial exchanges remarkably well.

August 1, 1955

Dear Jimmy,

or dear office of the dean of the university, whoever you are, greetings: not only from me, but from the familiars in the community—Elizabeth Shepley Sergeant (everybody and nobody's mother) and Esther Williamson Ballou (who saw your play in Washington and thought it marvelous) and others.

It's been unbearably hottest, but your manuscript went off to Beacon with a few minor changes. There are some larger matters we might quarrel about or drink over or forget, but we'll do that before THE COLLECTED WORKS appears and Paula Maria writes the biography. For this book, enough.

Nota bene:

Page 1, line 8, reads "the third of August we drove.. " (the month changes from death to funeral)

Page 1, 2nd par., line 3 "fr it" changed to "spoils" which may be more appropriate.

Page 2, line 5, I have deleted the phrase "where nothing, as yet, is stratified" which detracts from meaning and might not even be true.

Page 3, line 11 from bottom, last word changed from "beautiful" to "handsome." You talk about his (father's) beauty in line above, where it is appropriate, but here the somewhat more masculine adjective fits the man among spears, etc.

Page 4, line 9, I have deleted "a single" which is redundant and has your comment straining for the point, which is sufficiently omniscient anyhow to pass for xixhfxdxddxhxking projection.

Page 4, 4 lines from bottom, I have deleted first word "unquiet" which rings falsely literary. Its absence lends force to the sentence.

Page 5, two lines from bottom, I changed "listened" to "eavesdropped" which helps the idea a bit, I think, and is more precise for the behavior of people-children.

Page 6, 9 lines from bot, changed "taking me out" to "taking me to the theatre." Taking out sounds too much like a boy-girl date, which this was not.

Page 7, mid-page, sentence starting "Later" now begins a new paragraph.

Page 10, lines 2-3, have deleted phrase "which my veins were, daily, pumped full of poison. Or as though it were the year in" . Each time I read the essay I stopped over the image, which sounds too melodramatic.

Same page, 2nd par, 1st line, "A New York, white friend" now reads "a white friend from New York." Other is awkward.

Page 11, l. 4, "the diner" instead of "his diner"

Page 12, l. 3, deleted "which was even whiter now than usual" The "now" is bad intrusion of very present tense in past description. Whole phrase not needed; what not needed, prune.

Same page, 1st par. 2nd line end reads "like a thousand bells of a nightmare," which sounds better than the "nightmare bells."

Page 20, 1st line deleted "colored" which in context of this piece has immediate association of Negro and blurs your image.

Same page, l. 12-13 now reads "Then the house was suddenly full of relatives..." which gets rid of your "absolutely hideous" which is absolutely hideous. I know how you feel about them, but you're not hating them here, but describing wot happened.

Next line, I inserted quickly to read "and I quickly left my mother..."

Page 21, last line of top paragraph reads "I made my way to my father's funeral." You use "got", which is sloppy word anyhow, too often in this piece.

Same page, 4 lines further down, I inserted "onetime" to read "the faces of my father's onetime friends" because earlier you say that his friends didn't come to see him during the last period of his life.

Page 22, 9th line from bot, last word now reads "Every man..." because you've got his as a reference in next line.

Page 25, line 4, now reads "I was, at about this time..." Other phrase was awkward and uncertain.

Page 26, line 11, you had "He was simply a corpse, an old man dead.. " I deleted "a corpse," which, I think overdoes it. Without it, "an old man dead" becomes a beautiful phrase.

Page 31, last three lines, I reversed "he" in third line from bottom and "my father" from second line from bottom. Noun should come before pronoun to avoid confusion, especially at very end.

That's all for piddling points. If you don't like what I suggest, change 'em back, some or all, in proof. I promised not to deal with larger points, but I wish you would reconsider ~~two~~ two items on the last page (which I have not changed). The second idea was of "equal power." Not quite clear to me. Do you mean equal power as between whites and negroes? Also, I really don't like last line and a half, which sound like they were written by someone at the MacDowell Colony. His _face_ wouldn't tell you more now than it did then. Is what you mean that your heart was heavy because, now that your father was irrecoverable (very good word, by the way), you wished that he had been beside you so that you could have accepted him as he was? Please give some thought to this last sentence and, if you can, recompose for the proofs....which please correct promptly.

Must rush off to get this into the Peterborough mail. I want to talk to you about this chapter...after the book is out. It rocked me.

I never curse you and I don't know how to pray for you, but we both love you and wished you showed some signs of loving yourself, which you should, because nice people aren't writers and you are both in extremis.

August 23, 1955

Delaying publication of *Notes of a Native Son* by a month to accommodate a first serial sale continued to generate tension. Of course, what mattered most at the time was the extra money that the *Harper's* sale would provide for Baldwin and the possibility that the preview of a very strong chapter in *Harper's* could swell the audience for the book. As to the play of mine that I had to cut twenty pages out of overnight, I don't remember which play it was or where the reading was held. (A reading is usually done by actors with scripts in their hands.) Theater is a communal enterprise. Baldwin and I both eventually made the transition to the less stressful occupation of writing books, though Jimmy's lust to see his work on stage outlived mine.

NOTES OF A NATIVE SON

MacDowell Colony
Peterborough, New Hampshire
August 23, 1955

Mr. James Baldwin
46 W. 131 St.
New York, N. Y.

Dear Jimmy,

I was able to reach Mel Arnold in Boston by late morning, and lucky that I did: he was just about to take off for Detroit for a week. I OK'd the postponement of pub date on the book to November 10th and he agreed; I also suggested they take an ad in the November Harper's for the book. If he didn't have time to get off a note to your agent before leaving for Detroit, this letter will serve as authorization to go ahead.

Am nursing an awful summer cold (both the children went through this last week) with vodka, vitamins, and prayers, and last minute revisions for the reading tomorrow night (I had to cut 20 pp from Act II, hence the postponement). The New Dramatists Guild contract is awful, but the lawyers told me not to pretend I could read and to go ahead and sign, which I did. If I had read far enough I'm sure I would have found a clause that requires the author now to sit near the box office with a tin cup and a sign reading "Please feed the playwright."

I'll talk to you on the 31st, and we'll all see you soon afterwards.

                    Cheers,

                    Sol

September 1, 1955

The published version of *Notes of a Native Son* read fine half a century ago and still does. An index of *Notes of a Native Son* didn't make sense. These essays are meant to be read one word after the other, the way the author laid them on the page.

The "Trilling galleys" refers to Lionel Trilling's short book called *Freud and the Crisis of Our Culture*. Just a very few years earlier, I'd been a student in the Ph.D. seminar that Trilling gave (with Jacques Barzun) at Columbia University. When we sat down to go over my editing, Trilling said to me, "This will be more comfortable for both of us if we think of it that I taught you how to edit me."

"Lionel," I said, "the brain is an organ and the mind is the function of that organ, and you've got it ass backward through-out the book."

He taught me well. He also rewarded me two years later by writing a short article about me for the *Playbill* of a play of mine that was about to open on Broadway. Editing sometimes has ancillary rewards.

MEMORANDUM

DATE September 1, 1955

TO Sol Stein **FROM** Janet Finnie /9.7.

SUBJECT NOTES OF A NATIVE SON

The three sets of galleys, plus the manuscript, went to you today by parcel post, special delivery. We trust that they will reach you tomorrow, and that you'll be able to get them to the author.

Because it is a short book, do you think you and he could get your corrections back to us by Tuesday or Wednesday or next week?

One set of galleys contains a few queries for you. In the essay "Notes of a Native Son," you made a few changes in wording. In three of these places it was our opinion that the author's original version should stand. We've marked the spots, so that you may discuss them with the author if you feel strongly.

Have you thought about an index for this book? We'd like to have one; the index that Fiedler prepared for his collection of essays adds a good deal to the usefulness of his book.

Franz Hess informs Bob that the Trilling galleys should reach us to-morrow. We'll immediately forward a set to the author in Westport; and if all goes well he should receive them on Saturday. We'll send a set to you also -- to your office unless we hear to the contrary...

BEACON PRESS, 25 BEACON ST., BOSTON 8, MASS.

This is the jacket copy I wrote for *Notes of a Native Son*. The handwritten note at the top of the first page would suggest that Baldwin and I were to meet to go over this copy, which makes sense since the language and content are intended for the same audience as the essays themselves. I have no memory of that meeting, but there exists an undated letter to me from Baldwin that would indicate that he suggested changes in my copy and then withdrew those changes. While we were not of one mind, we would seem to have been on the same track. I don't know what happened up at the Beacon Press afterward, but flap copy is the province of the publisher, and an entirely different and deplorable version was printed on the flaps of the hardcover book. In rereading the flaps in 2002, I could not remember worse copy in my long publishing experience. Fortunately, the most important reviewers never saw those flaps and presumably reviewed the book from bound galleys that had no jacket, and based their reviews on the content of the book and not on the flaps.

I was wrong about the cup of coffee. It was a water glass, flung at the waitress who refused him service. It missed her and broke the mirror behind the bar.

In Baldwin's response, "See what Mr. K. thinks" probably

refers to Elia Kazan, to whom Baldwin may have sent a copy of his play *The Amen Corner*. Both Baldwin and I were friends of Kazan. I edited and published Kazan's *America America, The Arrangement*, and other successful books of his.

"L." refers to Lucien Happersberger, who was Baldwin's lover.

Jacket copy for James Baldwin's NOTES OF NATIVE SON

As <u>Commentary</u> said, James Baldwin's <u>Go Tell it on the Mountain</u>
"may be the most important novel yet written about the American Negro."
Similarly, Mr. Baldwin's present book is likely to be considered the most
important work of non-fiction on the same subject.

Baldwin can make mistakes, but he cannot lie. His book will therefore
earn the hatred of many Negroes and of those white people who are professional
champions of Negroes. Moreover, his experience of America will be a wet rag
flung across the face of Europe's intellectuals; his experience of Europe
will trouble Americans who think that for the dispossessed black man Paris
or Switzerland can be a possible home.

As a boy of seventeen, when Baldwin he was once refused service in a
Northern restaurant, Baldwin picked up a coffee cup and crashed it into the
mirrored wall. Like most other Negro writers, his rage turned into a credo.
Now, at 30, deriving his strength not from rage But from a precise intelligence,
his mind moves like a glasscutter over the events of his life/ and the culture
of his country.

Says Baldwin, "In the context of the Negro problem neither whites nor
blacks , for excellent reasons of their own, have the faintest desire to look
back; but I think that the past is all that makes the present coherent, and further,
that the past will remain horrible for exactly as long as we refuse to assess it
honestly.

"It is time for white people to stop feeling guilty about Negroes, and for
Negroes to stop trying to make them feel guilty, unless they want to feel
guilty about being persons on this earth. Guilt is a useless emotion, a way of
evading the responsibility of recognizing the existence of love. That love between
us began when some Uncle Tom somewhere found he loved his master a little,
making him that much less an Uncle Tom. Americans have a unique and valuable

others.

experience to offer ~~thexmxxixixtxtxpxexixnxixxxxxxixxxx~~ No other people

has ever been so deeply involved in the lives of black men, and vice versa.

It is precisely this black-white experience which may prove of indispensable

value to us in the ~~xixxxixx~~ world we face today. ~~Ixtxxxxixt~~ This world is white

no longer, and it will never be white again."

*****

James Baldwin was born in Harlen in 1924, the oldest of ~~eight~~ nine children

and the son of an (indeterminate father.) He ~~xxx~~ lived in Paris for six years

and has had no other profession save writing. The recipient of Saxton, Rosenwald,

and Guggenheim fellowships, he published his first novel (Go Tell it on the Mountain,

Alfred A. Knopf) ~~iznijx~~ in 1953. His ~~fzix~~ first play, The Amen Corner, was

produced at Howard University, Washington, in May of 1955.

clergyman

Dear Sol :

Any corrections I may have attempted in the blurb
copy you can feel free to ignore, allowing your copy to
stand as is. After a good deal of fruitless worry, I've
decided that the only way to avoid genuine misunderstanding
is to be as precise as possible in my text.

Have hunted high and low through Owen's library,
but 'Everybody's Protest' is all I can find. And, apparently,
I'm in great demand at the Howard Library. See what Mr. K.
thinks.

Will send up 'Notes' in a couple of days.But am
still a little dizzy with terror about my introduction to
such an excellent book. However -

Isn't the Cunard strike beautifully timed? If it
goes on much longer, L. is likely to lose a lung and America's
likely to lose a writer. (Just as soon not have it common
knowledge about L's illness, probably ought tohave said this
before).

Pray for me.

Jimmy

September 18, 1955

This book is about a friendship, and it was as a friend that I received the manuscript of Baldwin's novel *Giovanni's Room,* and as a friend that I gave him my views. I couldn't contemplate continuing as Baldwin's formal editor and quasi-publisher. Beacon did not as a rule publish fiction, my relationship with the press changed when the management changed, and I was still seven years away from founding my own book publishing firm, Stein and Day, which is really the first time I was employed full time as a publisher of books.

September 18, 1955

Mr. James Baldwin
c/o Mary Painter
8 rue des Carmes
Paris 5e, France

Dear Jimmy:

I have just finished reading GIOVANNI'S ROOM in one sitting, the
first time in many years I've read a novel in one sitting. It's very much
tighter than GO TELL IT; the first was a sweeping summary of everything
begun before GIOVANNI'S ROOM and this novel is a single bright flash of the
present. In writing GO TELL IT, you knew what would come after; here the
novelist doesn't know any more than the person writing the novel. The ir-
resolution is still a tangled sheet, beautiful for the novel, frightening
because it so much parallels the last conversation here in the office before
you left. Novels of the genre generally distort reality by simplifying.
Here there is no simplicity except the fine line that takes the story from
beginning to end. The crucial paragraph, I suppose, is the middle one, Page 89,
beginning "Then I alone..." If it weren't so terribly abstract, one might
almost call the novel"the question of my life."

In case you ever decide to do anything more with this, I have a few
small comments for your waste basket. I think you have to give Hella more
than you do. In the first few pages, you paint too hostile a portrait of her.
We have no reason yet to understand hostility. In any case, the hostility
should not be the author's. She is better than that. On the bottom of
P. 175, this is a very important moment for her-- and you have to give her
everything at this point, her speech has to be high and great, and this will
raise the level of the coming climax. On P. 175, Hella has to resound with
all of the eternal terror of womahood, but instead you explain her situation
instead of making it immediate. She can't say "Please let me be a woman."
We have to realize that this is what she is driving at by other, concrete
words that she says about herself and David. P. 96, you have four categories
of women: whores, virgins, minks and ice. You can't simplify David's enemy
this way, because he loves her also. She is not really any of these. She's
just as real as you are.

If you see what I mean by the above, you'll also see why I think that
the dialogue at the top of page 7 is so much soap-operaish.

At the tope of page 8, your transition "perhaps she is drinking now"
is the most powerful transition I ever remember reading.

Why should Joey be dark and brown?

On Page 33 the big fish eating little fish is a bit reminiscent of Hemingway's small opus. Besides, isn't it really a very simple metaphor for what is really a complicated situation? Page 46, shoot me but the plural of roof is roofs.

Jacques' small speech which starts at the bottom of 58 and ends at the top of 59 deserves a special medal. At the bottom of Page 66 you talk about "people I would never understand." I don't believe that of David. Or you. It would be easier if you didn't understand.

At the tope of Page 81, it's too much like a summary, and also not clear as to just what is happening. It sounds as if you tried to take a shortcut here. It probably could be cleaned up very easily.

Lest I forget, the scene between David and the blonde puffy girl both in the cafe and later in her room is superb. The universality of that scene is enough reason for the last sentence of the novel to carry the phrase "the dreadful weight of hope."

On Page,108, when your hero says that he's unscrupulous, I don't believe that he believes that he's unscrupulous any more than you believe that your unscrupulous. Know it, or ignore it, but don't fake it.

One slight technicality which you would probably want to ignore. What Giovanni really pleaded guilty to is manslaughter, that is, killing someone in the heat of anger, not first degree murder, which in this country, at least, is the mortal crime. Maybe in France manslaughter is punishable by death. I feel like an accountant or a mathematician raising a question like that, but you know I'll never learn to keep quiet about practical things. If I don't believe it, I can at least preach it.

In some ways, this novel is a step elsewhere from GOTTELL IT, and that elsewhere, I think, closer to heaven. I can't help thinking that both Mary and your mother will read this book, and that to both of them it will be like reading something they have read before---which is one of the reasons why Americans, with their clumsy but true insights, put women instead of men on pedestals.

I _am_ praying for you.

The radiogram, a form of international telegram, probably strikes young people like some ancient artifact, but in the decades before e-mail this is how people might communicate if you couldn't reach someone by expensive transatlantic phone. My two names were squeezed together as one because RCA charged by the word. I disavow the handwriting. The content was probably dictated. The radiogram was sent to Baldwin in care of American Express in Paris. It was a self-explanatory cry for Baldwin's promised introduction to Arnold Rose's *The Negro in America,* which was by then affecting the publication of a series of books. There was a point in early December when Beacon was asking for its advance money back, and I had to pass that message on to the agent for the book.

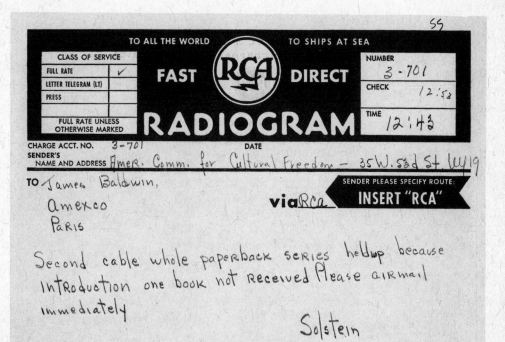

SS

TO ALL THE WORLD   TO SHIPS AT SEA

CLASS OF SERVICE	
FULL RATE	✓
LETTER TELEGRAM (LT)	
PRESS	
FULL RATE UNLESS OTHERWISE MARKED	

FAST RCA **DIRECT**

RADIOGRAM

NUMBER   3-701
CHECK   12:53
TIME   12:43

CHARGE ACCT. NO.   3-701   DATE

SENDER'S NAME AND ADDRESS   Amer. Comm. for Cultural Freedom — 35 W. 53d St. N/19

TO James Baldwin,
Amexco
Paris

via RCA

SENDER PLEASE SPECIFY ROUTE:
INSERT "RCA"

Second cable whole paperback series holdup because Introduction one book not received Please airmail immediately

Solstein

10100

Send the above Radiogram subject to the conditions, regulations and rates as set forth in the applicable tariff of RCA Communications, Inc., and on file with the regulatory authorities.

RCA COMMUNICATIONS, INC., A SERVICE OF RADIO CORPORATION OF AMERICA
(OVER)

This letter accompanied the typescript of the much-delayed first chapter of *Notes of a Native Son,* and probably dates from the summer of 1955, when Baldwin was having his play *The Amen Corner* produced at Howard University.

Dear Sol :

You can stop cursing me now. I hope.

The boy who had taken out the manuscript to mail the night I last talked to you didn't put enough stamps on it - I had told himto send it air-mail, special - so it came back. I was stuck in that hotel in Washington and wasn't even eating;

I couldn't tell this to the few people I know in Washington because they don't believe that such things happen. I eventually got my brother to bail me out and I'm at my mother's place in Harlem at the moment, being fattened up by my mother, according to her story, waiting for her to have an operation, according to mine. Her operation presents itself as more of a reality than my gaining weight.

Imporving the shining hour, meanwhile, by typing up the end of my hovel. Am in correspondence with London about my play. Lucien is gone, finally. I'm marking time until I get out of this greased well.

I hope you like the essay. I worked very hard on it, perhaps too hard. Cannot do Minority Report , cannot do anything new right now. Am clearing my desk of previous committments - people all over NY are bitter against me - and, that done, will pull myself together and go to see a doctor. Don't know what I'll do then, depends on what he says. But prefer to get the desk clear and see my mother safely in and out of the hospital before I further endanger my own morale.

OFFICE OF THE
DEAN OF THE UNIVERSITY .

Will write more another day. Give my love to Sonny
and the kids, and have a good summer.

Write me : 46 West 131st Street, NYC. Phone AU -3-2231

Love,

Jimmy

November 29, 1955

Paula is Baldwin's sister, to whom *Notes of a Native Son* was dedicated. The introduction Baldwin was late in delivering was for Arnold Rose's book, *The Negro in America*. The publisher gave up hope of receiving Baldwin's introduction and had Arnold Rose write his own preface. The last sentence of my letter refers to Baldwin's refrain, "God help me."

42-42 Gleane St.
Elmhurst 73, N. Y.
November 29, 1955

Dear Jimmy,

The enclosed reviews are from advance copies of the Dec. 5th
issue of TIME and NEWSWEEK.   Nora de Toledano helped me arrange
for the one in TIME. It was their principal review in that issue.

I suppose you know that the book is the Associated Press' "Book
of the Week," and that your face will appear in papers throughout the
country. (WANTED...etc)

Your mother and Paula spent half a day Sunday here with us and
the children. THEY are nice, as distinguished from at least one of their
relatives.

Caliban was a Jew. The introduction didn't come in, the book was
cancelled from the spring list, Harper's is mad, Beacon is mad, Mel Arnold
wants his $150 back fast, they are hardly on speaking terms with me, and
all because geniuses sometimes tell worse fibs than Joe McCarthy (RIP).
And now you and I are hardly on speaking terms, which is why this letter
is short.

        I tried to pray for you, but God said he didn't
        know where to find you.

                    Best,

                    Sol

P.S. Sunnie send her love, because women are always forgiving.

December 27, 1955

It is a fact of life that in theater as well as books, the review in
The New York Times can make or break a play or book. Here,
Harvey Breit of the *Times* tries to reassure me. His reference to
1984 is the film based on Orwell's book. I had no memory of
participation in that project, though correspondence from others confirms that I did. Orwell's *Homage to Catalonia,* which
was published in the same series as Baldwin's *Notes of a Native
Son,* was also selected as one of the "100 best nonfiction books
of the century."

THIS SIDE OF CARD IS FOR ADDRESS

BUILD YOUR FUTURE
WISELY
U.S. SAVINGS BONDS

POSTAL CARD

Sol Stein Esq.
35 West 53rd St.
New York 19. N.Y.

THE NEW YORK TIMES BOOK REVIEW
TIMES SQUARE   NEW YORK 36, N.Y.

27 Dec.

Dear Sol: There is nothing you need do. We have a fine review of Baldwin's book in type + it will run very soon now. It came in late & was held out for space reasons last week. Too bad about 188 f: it would have been a hell of a fine thing. Yrs,
Francis

January 9, 1956

This letter is how I first learned that Baldwin had had a nervous breakdown. As usual, it was undated, but it was received on January 9, 1956.

Dear Sol :

Back in my skin and back at my desk, and I
thought I'd better say something to you first.

But it's only a note, because there's too much
to say. First, this time, no shit, I'll get the intro
out to you, if not with this evening's mail, then in
the mail in the morning. This is not a semi-delirious
cable, but news, so to speak, from home.

I hope I don't need to say that I didn't intend
or expect that any of this would happen; I'd like to add
that it wasn't the money that did it; or at least I'd
like to think that. You, or whoever it was, may be right
about me, I don't know.

As for the rest : I thought I was sick, and
indeed I was, but it turned out to be only a breakdown.
About breakdowns, baby, there is nothing to say, nothing
one _can_ say while it's happening, nothing to be said when
it's over. Not even, I hope it will never happen again
for a breakdown, I've discovered - hindsight - can be a
most valuable thing.

Still - mine is over, it seems I want to live,
I'm working again, and I'll write you a real letter soon.

Please give my dearest love to Sunnie and to your
boys.

                                        Love,

                                        Jimmy

69

I suppose I wanted every possible reinforcement for my friend's first book of essays to succeed. For instance, the original paperback edition had a flyleaf listing the Beacon Contemporary Affairs Series and putting Baldwin into the company of prominent writers such as André Malraux, Eric Bentley, Sidney Hook, George Orwell, Arthur Koestler, Simone Weil, and Bertram D. Wolfe. It may have been a mistaken attempt at such reinforcement when I wrote a brief editor's prefatory note for the first hardcover edition of *Notes of a Native Son*. Perhaps I was haunted by the trade adage "Essays don't sell." The key word is *cohere*.

The prefatory note was set in type and included in the bound galleys because the *Library Journal* took note of it. However, before the book itself was on press, I asked Beacon to remove my prefatory note on the ground that who was I to approve of Baldwin's work except by my labors on its behalf.

In the jargon of writers, "pieces" is the word used
to describe articles, essays, and the uncategorizable writings
which constitute the writer's baggage while he is travelling
between major works. Yet of Lord Acton, for instance, such
"pieces" are all we have; fortunately, they inform each other
as well as us and constitute a whole. That is also the virtue
of James Baldwin's xxxxxxxx pieces, a frightening virtue in one
so young. They cohere, and that is apology enough for bringing
them together, that and the fact that when we consider the
concluding chapter of this book, "Stranger in the Village,"
and try to think of a greater essay ever written by a member
of Mr. Baldwin's race, we cannot name it.

S.S.

[handwritten note: How does this strike you... is best of an introduction for

February 27, 1956

This carbon copy is a letter by me. I was trying to get Baldwin additional writing assignments. "Letter to My Younger Brother" was intended for a series of inexpensive hardbound individual essays. The earliest became classics—Lionel Trilling's *Freud and the Crisis of Our Culture* and Daniel Bell's *Notes on Work*.

The original director of the Beacon Press was Melvin Arnold, with whom I had an excellent rapport and who published my series of trade paperbacks in the very early days of that format. As a result of the series, Melvin Arnold became first the director of the religious books department at Harper & Row and then its president.

Baldwin was notoriously late in delivering material.

February 27, 1956

Mr. James Baldwin
119 Avenue des Versailles
Paris 16, France

Dear Jimmy:

Thomas Bledsoe, an editor at Knopf, is taking over the directorship of Beacon Press on April 1. We spoke this morning and he mentioned the long-delayed introduction to the Arnold Rose book. (Apparently he knows Rose well and will be seeing him towards the end of this week.) The book was scratched from the current list of paperbacks, which are just out now, and I really don't know what to say to him about the prospects of deliveryoon the introduction.

There is also the matter of LETTER TO MY YOUNGER BROTHER, the essay for which you were to get $500 on delivery. Bledsoe is now scheduling the Mid-Century Series through the spring of 1957, and I am naturally leery about scheduling anything at this point. I believe that Trilling earned something like $1500 in royalties on copies sold in advance of publication and I should think this essay is something ;you would want to do. Also, you know that the government is very interested in quantity purchases of the volume.

Langston Hughes reviewed your book in yesterday's New York *Times Book Review*. I found it strange but everybody else seems to think it's a wonderful review and so my judgment is swept away by the majority. I called the review toyour Mother's attention. Sondra and I have both talked to her a number of times since her return from the South.

The play is still scheduled for an early fall opening, and I am working madly away at changes on the umpteenth revision.

Your agent has asked to see carbons of these letters, hence the exclusion of more personal matters...which I'll get to when I have a chance to write from home. In the meantime, Sondra and the children send their love.

Best,

cc: Helen Strauss

P.S. I have had word from Bledsoe that he has discussed with Arnold Rose the fact that there has been a half year delay in the receipt of the introduction and he has therefore asked me to advise you the Professor Rose has now been asked to do his own introduction and that the $150 advance to you will be deducted from royalties on NOTES. I am truly sorry about this but I am afraid I can do very little about the business affairs of Beacon Press ;other than to hurry an advance, as I did last September. Please write to me soon about LETTER TO MY YOUNGER BROTHER.

These undated, unpublished notes for a new project are an important statement by Baldwin of his views.

I had suggested to Baldwin that he might want to do an essay for the Mid-Century Series I was editing for Beacon. I recently found a copy of his notes for such a book, which he called "Letter to My Younger Brother." David Baldwin was close to Jimmy throughout his life and was a friend of mine as well. During the late '50s or early '60s David and I worked together. We last touched hands over the roof of the car in which Berdis Baldwin sat as she waited to be driven from the funeral of her eldest son.

Notes for project, <u>Letter To My Younger Brother</u> .

Author actually has a younger brother, David, recently returned from military service in Korea, and Japan. The controlling tone of this essay - which will not be in the form of a letter - is dictated by the need to affirm for this brother, despite the upheavals he is certain to witness - and endure - in his own lifetime, not only a certain standard of human and personal dignity, but also the incessant need for clarity.

The essay is tentatively divided into three parts. The first is an informal and interpretative glance at the history of the Negro in this country; this, in order to convey to David a sense of his own history in this country, to give him an awareness of his ancestors, and of distances covered, ax sense, in short, of his own place in this long line from slavery to difficult and ambiguous freedom.

The second part is a glance at David's life until the present moment - an evaluation, that is, of the last twenty years. This section is not predominantly sociological and isn't written with the intention of giving David any easy comfort. Rather, it is meant to be specific, to throw into some kind of perspective those things which have happened to him, and which he has seen. These things have often not been pretty, nor will they be prettied up, for the good reason that such an attempt can only add to David's bitterness. I would like, if I may so put it, to rid David of the notion that he is a victim. Such a notion can only cause him to despise all Negroes and all whites and such a notion will prevent him from seeing or understanding any of the forces which have shaped, and are shaping his life. In this discussion,

I also want to talk about the forces which have been awakening and stirring in the East and in Africa during the last two decades, the impact on the world of the Russian Revolution, and the meaning - not only for David'. - of the end of Western imperialism. I hope this does not sound too far-fetched: these things will be discussed in the hardest and homeliest terms possible.

The third section is a kind of wedding of the first two, more difficult to sum up because it necessarily involves speculation about the future. It may be said, anyway, that the citizenship of the American Negro in the West is taken as a _fait accompli_; the struggle before David will be less the winning of his place in the West than the realization of what this place is, and what it means, and waht it demands of him. One of the things it will surely demand is a new and very painful awareness of his far-flung darker brother, whose relationship to the white world is not, whatever they, or David may be tempted to believe, analogous to the American Negro's relationship. But it will also demand a new and very painful awareness of white men, and his relationship to them : it will not be possible to choose sides, since David is, by now, both white and black. This position is unique and it is, perhaps, the point of the essay, and my own belief, that ,if rightly understood and lived through, it can lead to an achievement as unique in its own way as the yet-to-be-recorded achievement of the Negro in the United States.

James Baldwin

April 8, 1956

This letter is a carbon copy of a letter I sent to Baldwin. The introduction referred to is the one that was commissioned but never received for Arnold Rose's *The Negro in America*.

The "Witness" referred to was a best-selling book by Whittaker Chambers. The Theater Guild commissioned me to write a play based on it. I eventually wrote a play from the public record and called it *A Shadow of My Enemy*, which was produced on Broadway in 1957 thanks to Roger Stevens, Alfred de Liagre Jr., and Hume Cronyn, with Nick Mayo as producer. Lionel Trilling wrote an article about me for the *Playbill* of *A Shadow of My Enemy*.

April 8, 1956

Dear Jimmy,

This is in answer to your long March letter about the introduction. You didn't give me a raw deal. It may be easier for you to say that, so let it stand. But it is still yourself that you are giving raw deals to (punishment for what, Caliban?), but that's harder to say. We "expect" to treat others roughly but not ourselves, whom we supposedly love, and if the evidence has it that we don't behave appropriately about our self-love, it cries for some difficult answers. I've begun to learn just a few of these, four times a week for an hour. I don't recommend it to anyone looking for a pastime. It's a hell decorated by Cocteau, peopled by the tenants of infancy we'd rather forget, and supervised by the damndest person--who only listens, and lets you do all the work. Things get better, then terribly worse, andxxxx sometimes worse because you end up looking in other peoples' dark closets as well as your own, and up your mother's skirt, and into the toilet to see if it's really a little priest that you got rid of (that's an Eastern European Jewish explanation to children of why people look back after they're through on the pot).

Everyone with intålligence loves Notes (with some frequency I've heard it compared favorably with your novel-- "Why this man writes like a 19th century English don; he's so damn precise about his huge emotions"). But it's not selling too terribly well...enough to cover the advance, however. You should make some money on the paperback edition that's planned for fall.

What's happened with Giovanni's Room, meaning novel, Lucien, and habit?

Violent upheavals here. Quitting the Committee and several of my much too many jobs and taking one, one only, where I'll be able to serve my 35 hours of penance each week and devote the rest of the time to writing. Psychoanalysis helped that much at least. More. As for "Witness," it's almost nothing at all like what you read. Trilling said it's got a classic simplicity and depth now, and two giants who lock antlers inextricably, like stags doomed to die because they cannot separate their battle.

We're having another baby. If you come back and be its godfather....anything to tempt you home. Behold what wrongs our Prometheus endures...I can't mock it; it's the greatest single line in Greek drama. Come home, Jimmy, we've got a great big plymouth rock to tie you to, if that's what you want. It's what we want, even if we have to make a great American rock out of paper mache to attract you. Don't you know how boring practically everbody is without you?

Love from all of us,

November 9, 1956

Baldwin sent this letter from Corsica. The novel he was working on was *Another Country.* Daniel Bell, the sociologist and
later a distinguished professor at Harvard, was the author of
Notes on Work, which I had edited and published at the
Beacon Press. The new job was as Managing Editor at the
Research Institute of America, and the new house was my first,
located in Forest Hills, in the fourth-floor garret of which,
some months later, Baldwin and I worked on the story and play
in this book. The new baby's name, Leland Dana, was a subject
that later amused us both. *Letter to My Younger Brother* was
originally conceived as a letter to Baldwin's closest brother
David. In a later letter in this book, I comment on *Princes
and Powers.*

Dear Sol :

postmarked Nov 9
'72

Long time no contact. And very
glad to re-establish it.

Thing go on with me in what I
suppose I must, by now, break down and call
the usual fashion. I've spoiled a lot of
paper since I last saw you, hated myself –
but perhaps rather less than usual! is that
(he demanded nervously) a good sign? – am
in a great house now, on an island, all alone,
working on what I trust will be the final
draft of the new novel. Can't wait to get
off this island, I know exactly how Napoleon
must have felt – and I also observe that he
died on an island – plus ça change! etc–
and when I do, I'll be coming home. To
tell the truth, I had hoped to be home by
now. But if I don't finish this novel now
I never will; and on this novel, as far as
I'm concerned, all future novels depend.

So much for all that. As for
all this, well – I've come to the end of a
great many things. I don't know if that's good
or bad, certainly can't talk about it in a
letter. All it seems, anyway, to add up to
is that I've alot of work to do. Can't do
anything if I don't do that, nothing good

will ever come of me - if I don't do that. And
stated that way, it sounds fearfully obvious,
banal, something, one would say, which I
must always have known. All I can say is
that it's astonishing how many times the
same, banal cup comes round.

Oh , well. Heard, through
Dan Bell, about your new job, new house;
didn't hear, however, about the new baby.
Which must have been born by now. Please
let me know how and what it is, name, and
how Sunny is. Kiss her for me. Kiss the
three children for me, too.

Letter To My Younger Brother
has been suffering from my ignorance concerning Africans; an ignorance which I've
now decided to utilize, for I will never
really understand any more of Africa than
the insights afforded me by some of the
Africans I meet. More than that, though,
it's suffered from a certain, unsuspected
condescension I've got in me towards Africans.
This can't be defended, and I'll probably never
entirely overcome it. It was a shock. Just
the same, I wish you'd have my agent show
you Princes and Powers, the report I've just
done for Endounter, on the Conference of Negro-
African Writers and Artists which was held in
Paris in Sptember. It mirrors my confusion,

certainly, but it also mirros theirs. Letter
will begin where thid ends, and I hope to
have it finally written when I come home-
I'm more convinced of its importance than I
was before. (I imagine I'll be coming home
around March; it depends on the novel; will
let you know).

Well, there's too much to say.
Will say it to you, in person, on one of the
four living levels of your new house.

In the meantime, keep in
touch.

Love to you all,

Jimmy

Case postal 20
Ile Rousse,
Corsica

Baldwin's sister Gloria was his secretary for years. She is now known as Gloria Baldwin Karefa-Smart and is the Executor of the James Baldwin Estate. The story he was writing, first published in *Partisan Review,* was "Sonny's Blues." Note that at the age of thirty-two Baldwin says of his novel in progress, "Hope I live to see it," and of the jazz story, "I thought it would be the death of me." These common phrases about death, usually sloughed off, are characteristically about his work, which did not come easily.

Dear Sol :

I think I've written you this
before, perhaps a couple of years ago : my
good friend, Mary Painter, is coming to NY -
is in NY as you read this - and will be
getting in touch with you. If I have
written you this before, nothing came of
it, because you haven't yet met; but you
will this time, I think, for one thing
Mary may be staying in NY. For another,
                her
I told/you'd give her a copy of <u>Notes</u>.
We met in Nice for a few days to say au
revoir and in my usual scatter-brained
fashion I came away without any of the
addresses I was supposed to give her,
including yours. Either she'll try to
get in touch with you through the American
Committee, or she'll wait to hear from
me. But she had to write me first, I don't
know where she'll be staying.

Anyway, be nice to her. I don't
think it will be hard to nice to her, in fact ,
I should think it would be hard not to. As
I may have told you, she's shy. I think
she'll like Sunny. Also, I don't know if she's
going to go straight to her family in Minneap

olis and spend time in NY on her way back, or
vice-versa. But she'll probably let me know
and I'll let you know.

Another thing : my sister, Gloria,
who has just had her third child, has been
deserted by her husband, who refuses to pay
anything toward the support of the children
and insists on a divorce. (He's quit his
job and left the city). My mother writes
me about it, and asks me if I know of a
lawyer. Well, I don't. But I told her to
get in touch with you, I hope you don't
mind, I couldn't think of anyone esle
whomight have concrete suggestions to
offer, as well as, perhaps, a kind of
moral boost. In a way, it's just as well
that Gloria's rid of the man - he's a
no-good little shit - but it's a hard
moment for her. I'm doing what I can from
here in the way of money and moral support, but
all things legal are for them a kind of
threatening mystery. Sound reassuring. (If
Mama doesn't call you, please call her; Au-
3-2231).

I hate to burden you with
my family but I consider that they're
really much nicer than I am.

The n ew novel shows occasional

signs of turning into one one of these fine days. Hope I live to see it. And finishing, at last! a short story about jazz which I thought would be the death of me - I've been struggling with it for over a year. I still don't know if it's any good but I know I can't do anything more with it. I think it'll be in PR presently, that is, as soon as I mail it. Oh, well.

It will be nice to see the homestead again. It would be even nicer if I could feel that I'd ever feel at home there. I'll tell you this, though, if you don't feel at home at home, you never really feel at home. Nowhere. I try to keep remembering something Peter Viereck told me, simply that you don't live where you're happy or, for that matter, unhappy : you do your best to live where you can work.

See you soon. Take care of you and yours.

Jimmy

December 10, 1956

This letter is out of chronological order. It crossed in the mail with my letter of December 7, 1956, which belongs together with Baldwin's reply.

12-10-56

Dear Sol :

A note, to give you Mary
Painter's New York address, in case she's
not managed to reach you. She's staying at
419 West 118th Street, NYC, c/o Teutsch.

I'm working very hard, but
am terribly behind o n magazine committments.
That's because I got side-traaked by a long
stretch on the novel, and then by a short
story. Have torn up the long stretch and
mailed the short story, so I suppose things
are more or less back to normal.

I intend to write you a letter
before Xmas, and possibly actually will;
but just in case, let me wish you and yours
a merry Christmas and a Happy New Year, and
well, much, much more than that.

Kiss Sunnie and the children,
and God bless you all.

As ever,

The following letters, mine of December 7, 1956, and Baldwin's response that refers to his leaving Corsica for the holidays, suggest a date in early 1957 for his reply. Baldwin's letter first takes care of "business," the play *Equal in Paris,* but quickly segues into themes that were part of our occasional differences. Prescient about America's present role in the world, he said, "America is the last stronghold of the Western idea of personal liberty. And I certainly think that this idea *should* dominate the world [Baldwin's emphasis]. But one of the ways in which it will do so, if it does, is through politics. And I have certainly very bitterly wished that we were better politicians than we are, and had more faith in our own ideals."

Baldwin's comments about W.E.B. Du Bois and civil liberties are in reply to my strangely split position at the time. In the early and mid-'50s, Baldwin and I were both involved with the American Committee for Cultural Freedom, which opposed denial of passports to any citizen. The Soviet Union enslaved a significant portion of its own citizens and was a twentieth-century slave state. I believed that Du Bois's praise of the Soviet Union was inappropriate for an opponent of slavery. Prior to this correspondence, the U.S. State Department had deprived Du Bois of his passport and his ability to travel abroad. I came to view the withholding as wrong, but there are rare circumstances in which a passport might need to be withheld, for instance, a convicted felon might use a passport to flee the country, as some have, or a fleeing terrorist suspect may have information that might help avoid further terrorist attacks. Such exceptions should be extremely rare and determined by a proper and quick judicial review, not by State Department or law enforcement officials. Passports should never be withheld, in my judgment, for opinions or views.

Baldwin's reference in the penultimate paragraph is to my first wife and three of our children.

December 7, 1956

Dear Jimmy:

First things first. I've been trying to reach your mother and am
told I can get to her tonight. I'll try to arrange for a lawyer on the
family situation, perhaps something more if it seems appropriate. You
say all things legal are for them a kind of threatening mystery. Them?

Mary Painter called and I'll be seeing her next week.

Glad you're coming home, though Peter Viereck is wrong when he says
that you don't live when you're happy or unhappy; you live where you can
work. It's more complex than that. I had a call from Peter just at a-
bout the time that your letter arrived. His fine work seems in the past,
his ivory tower has twenty ramparts down any of which he is ready to
charge at a moment's notice. He devotes frantic energies at trying to
make ends meet on a professor's salary -- would in a sense break up his
family to do so by having his wife live in another town because she can
get work there. Work is not a penalty.

As for you, do you know that work is not a penalty or a necessary
source of pay? It's not a punishment; you settled that one with the
preacher long ago. Work is what you do when you can, which means when
you're not earning a living, or loving a family, or doing the things that
come first -- even if work is ultimately more important. If you'd recog-
nize the when factor, maybe you'd stop running all around the world looking for the where. When you've made some real peace with yourself, your
old man and the white world, the where will fall back into its proper
place; an environment, and that's all.

The baby's name is Leland Dana. An old Hebrew name.

Your piece "Princes and Powers". It's not par, especially the long
beginning. It reads too much like a working paper for a piece rather than
the piece itself. When Eliot says "notes toward a definition of culture",
he's protecting himself unnecessarily. These are notes.

The writing is not as uniformly good as I've come to expect of you. Neither is the thinking. Russia and America are not battling for the domination of the world. That's an inaccuracy and all I am quarreling with here is inaccuracy. As for DuBois, when you have a teenager with an eight year old mentality who likes to go down to a certain neighborhood every Saturday night and almost always comes back either cut up or with a case of VD, if you're the parent you sometimes reach the point where you don't let him out anymore. It's nice to be able to say "The hell with it. If he wants to go, let him." How can you say it though when everyone identifies him as a member of your family rather than as a crazy kid. That's America's problem with DuBois. You look at it much too much in terms of black and white, and I thought you didn't particularly care for those colors.

By the way, if the Asians think it's a necessity to remake the world in their own image and to impose this image on the world, it will be over my dead body. Most Asians, which means most colored people, have -- I suppose out of necessity or because of their culture -- a morality that is basically cynical. The cynicism sticks even when they get educated at Oxford (e.g. Nehru, Menon, Badaranaike). Hypocracy is also a dominant Asian trait. The concept of "face" is certainly not comparable to the understanding of, let us say, Freudian Psychology. We have a tremendous and unjustified inferiority here in the West. I think we are going to be eradicated by the Asians. But as I said, over my dead body. Please think of that when you write about it. The Chinese and just, the Hungarians revolt.

These comments are incomplete and unfair insofar as they are incomplete. But how much time should we waste in praise. I think "Letter to My Younger Brother" will have to be a lot more accurate than this and much more polished simply in terms of the writing. As an editor, I am sure Maxwell Perkins was kinder than I am, but then he was dealing with Thomas Wolfe and I am not dealing with quantity.

One thing more, and this important. Daniel Petrie, the man who will be directing my play this spring and I are trying to buy the rights, or a year's option on doing either a movie or TV show or both of "Equal in Paris". With a lot of help, we could swing this. I have insisted that you should get some participation in the eventual movie, if one is made, rather than a flat fee now. You would, of course, get some kind of nominal payment now as an advance. Could you light a fire under your agent on this subject? At least 50% of this proposition will be in hands you ought to be able to trust by now and something good all around might come of it. May I suggest you write both to Helen Strauss and to me about this just as soon as you can.

Love from everyone,

SS/rs

Dear Sol :

I left Corsica for the holidays,
which allows me to find Corsica charming once
again, an attitude which will, I hope, carry
me through till May. Before I left this island,
though, I did set a fire under my agent re-
garding your 'Equal In Paris' proposition,
and I supposed that the two of you had already
gottten together about it. I simply repeated
your proposition, and added that I had all
kinds of confidence in you, and that the sooner
something was done about the deal, the better.
I am writing her in the same mail as this, and
will repeat myself. I have already suggested
that she call you. I will now suggest that
you call her.

I didn't write you, though, because
I've been thinking over your last long letter to
me - the one in which you tell me that 'work is
not a penalty' and take issue with some of the
things in Princes and Powers. As for the writing
and the fact that they are notes, I agree - but
I wonder about some other questions -

First things first, however, and
getting back to that 'work is not a penalty'
notion, I have it on the highest Western authority
that this was exactly how it entered the world.

(see Genesis). But, as a matter of fact, I
agree that work is not a penalty, or cannot,
in any case, be considered as one; yet, when
you say that work is what you do _when_ you
can - when not earning aliving, loving a
family, 'doing the things that come first' -
I'm lost. Suppose work _is_ earning a living
and also - _faute de mieux_, perhaps - loving
a family, suppose work _is_ first, simply
because, for a particular life, nothing else
can possibly come without it? What then?
I don't, myself, think that I've seriously
considered work as a penalty, though I _do_
consider it my only means of understanding
the world, and, in fact - at the risk of
causing you to gnash your teeth- my only
means of feeling at home in the world. I
don't know what Ithink until I've writtenx
it. Voila. I'm not trying to/flippant. Think
about it. And I insist on this a little out
of consideration for our friendship : though
I, personally, am sure that you will one day
see me as safe and happy as any friend of mine
could wish, this day will not be tomorrow and
work, my friend, is my only means of bringing
this day about. _Please_ get over the notion, Sol,
that there's some place I'll fit when I've made
some 'real peace' with myself : the place in

which I'll fit will not exist until I make it .
You know and I know that the 'peace' of most
people is nothing but torpor, and you also
know that there is no such thing as an 'external
enviromment and that's all'. An enviromment is
also an inward reality, it's one of the things
which makes you, it takes from you and it gives
to you, facts which are suggested by the word
itself. If I were trying to escape my environment, I wouldn't be covering the earth to do
it. The best way to escape one's environment
is to surrender to it. I, personally, am trying
to understand mine, in which endeavor I may
possibly be retarded - but I don't think I'm
romantic enough, any loner, to imagine that
anything is ever escaped.

Well. All the above's inadequate.
We'll pick it up over a drink sometime. As for
the piece: you say I'm inaccurate in saying
that America and Russia are battling for the
domination of the world. What, then, I wonder,
would be accurate? What else have nations ever
battled for? And it's no answer, you know, to
say that nations have battled, for example,
for the right to be left alone, or the right
to be free; small nations, with no realistic
hope of extending their influence, are content
(perhaps) with these blessings; large nations
never have been. Do you object to the word

'domination'? But domination is one of the facts of life, particularly in the present case: it is perfectly clear that if America is not dominant, Russia will be. I, personally, prefer to see America dominant (though I have great reservations about this as relates to the domestic life of our country, but this is another discussion altogether and a bridge to be crossed when reached). Politics _is_ involved with power, power raises questions of submission or domination. I don't see how this can be denied. In my sentence, I didn't, anyway, mean merely political domination - Russia has that in Hungary - but the domination of the minds of men. (England had this for many generations). By domination, in short, I did not mean bayonets, but the kind of domination which is achieved when the same idea becomes real in many lives. Think, for example, of the Christain doctrine; but remember, too, that the history of the church is bloody. I am not inventing paradoxes, friend, only observing them. In the case of America vs. Russia, America is the last stronghold of the Western idea of personal liberty. And I certainly think that this idea _should_ dominate the world. But one of the ways in which it will do so, if it does, is through politics. And I have certainly very

bitterly wished that we were better politicians
than we are, and had more faith in our own ideals.

Which brings me to DuBois. Your
metaphor, the teen-aged kid going out and
making scandals every Saturday night so that
the family eventually decided to keep him home,
simply does not work. DuBois is not a teenager, but a very old man, quite justly renowned
for his role in American Negro history, a role
he was playing against quite unimaginable odds
a long time before the Russian revolution. Dis-
agreeing with him completely, and very disappointed
by his present bitter irresponsibility, I can
yet see that this revolution must have meant
to him something it could not conceivably have
meant to you or me. Also, the world is not a
block, politics is not VD. It seems quite clear
to me that DuBois' own career, which is at least
as long as this century is old, is a very fine
piece of pro- American propaganda, and this
despite anything he can possibly say. The
fact is that he has lived long enough to see
the situation of the American Negro improved
beyond anything he could possibly have hoped
in 1900, he represents a minority report which
no other nation in the world can match. Refusing
to give him a passport serves no purpose whatever.
It simply plays into the hands of those Europeans

who are determined to distrust us – to speak
only of the Europeans – and embarasses everybody
else. What can DuBois possibly say which has
not already been said by the Associated Press?
His effect can scarcely be greater than the effect
of the photographs, in all the European papers
a few months ago, of Negro children arriving
at unwillingly desegregated Southern schools.

He can only add his own political beliefs;
which then become, however, nothing more or
less than his own political beliefs; which
can be challenged; what we have done is sanctify
them by what all the world is only toowilling
to acceptas martyrdom. If we believe in freedom,
honey, we got to take freedom's risks. And,
anyway, why stop at keeping DuBois at home?
Why not suppress the photographs, tailor
the stories – don't laugh. Whatever has
happened to people can happen to people
again.

As for the necessity of non-
Europeans to remake the world in their own
image and to impose this image on the
world – I don't doubt that it will be over
your dead body, and mine, too. The world
which they are making will not have any
room for us. The point, however, is that
they _are_ making this world; and there's

no point in being offended at their lack of
genrosity in wishing to impose their image of
the world _on_ the world; this is precisely what
Europe did to them and, as far as they are
concerned, this is almost the entire history
of the European civilszation. People donot
like to be ruled by strangers, they donot like
to be made to feel inferior . It cannot be
denied that Europeans, for them, were strangers,
not can it be denied that Eureope considred
them inferior - inferior because they fell
below the European standard , because they
did not fit into the European vision of
the world. The European civilization over-
ran and destroyed theirs, Europe's morals
and aesthetics invalidated their own. This
is the way, or one of the ways in which
'domination' works. There's no point in
being sentimental about this, one way or
the other, and still less point in blaming
them; particularly as one's not blaming them
for the desire, which was always there, but
simply for the fact that this desire cann, as
it now seems, be transformed into action. One
can only hope that they travel West, not East,
and do our best to seduce them into believing
in such things as _habeas corpus_. (Though it
cannot be said that we, in our dealings with

them, have been a very good example. There
are two Western civilizations, you know, the
one in which we live and the one other people
have been living outside of).

As for the cynicism of colored
peoples, I'm not altogether sure that I know
what you mean. (Though I can't resist pointing
out that non-Europeans think that Europeans -
watching the considerable gap between their
professions and their acts - are cynical).
imm I'm not sure, for example, that we're
inm any position to understand the concept
of 'face' - anyway, I certainly don't
understand it. You may mean the same thing
you mean when you say that hypocrisy is a
dominant Asian trait. (Which is a rather
large statement, I think, but let it pass).
I suggest, though, that it may have something
to do with the kind of mask they have been
presenting to white people for God knows
how many generatipns. I am sure that they
soon stopped trying to tell thetruth to a
white man. Perhaps now they can't. God help us
all.

But I've said too much and not
enough and it's late. I'll mail this in the
morning. Good- night.

Morning : apropos of the remarks

about DuBois, ones of the questions his
situation raises is the question of just
what a passport is:is it a privilege allowed
the government for some citizens? - if so,
this should be stated; or is it the right of
all citizens? In the latter case - which is
the way I believe it ought to be - then there
is simply no question but that the State Dep't.
is wrong. But if a passport is now to be considered a privilege, then this should be made
quite clear. Part of the confusion is caused
by the fact that no-one in authority, as far
as I know, has faced up to this question, or
its implications.

Enough for now. I'm working hard,
will be home soon. Give my love to Sunnie,
Kevin, Jeff, Leland Dana. (It must be a very
old Hebrew name).

My mother and my sister, by the
way, write that you've been very nice and helpful,
as I knew you would be. Thank you very much.

As ever,

Jimmy

April 3, 1957

"Equal in Paris" refers to the play that James Baldwin and I
wrote together for the Theater Guild's *U.S. Steel Hour*. The
story of this venture is included in the introductory essay.

April 3, 1957

Dear Jimmy,

I am writing this in heat, as they say. Got the word
this afternoon that our agents, after what seems like months
of dillying and wrangling, have come to terms, and I've been
excitedly making notes for the dramatization of EQUAL IN PARIS.
I talked to two producers just yesterday, both good prospects
if it works out right. One just made a film (good reviews, bad
film) with a Negro in the lead, so maybe it'll work in spite of
the reservations of Bill Fitelson and others aboutthe controversial
controversial controversial idea of EQUAL. (The bad film is a new
twist on Uncle Tom; the nice intelligent Negro befriends a real
shit of a white man, who isn't worth befriending, and dies
defending him; it was directed by a guy who, last I heard, was
a Communist...which fits.)

First off I'll make an hour TV show out of it. The fee
would be about $3000, if I'm lucky, and we split this 50/50
(that's what my agent screamed about; the usual is 70/30 or
60/40 in favor of the adaptor). The real monetary incentive,
of course, is the chance that the TV story might be bought for
the movies. Budd Schulberg is interested in getting Dan Petrie
to do one or more of the slew of films he expects to produce
abroad...and why not this one, in Paris.

I neglected your long and beautiful letter. Read it many
times, still do, but I have the feeling that when we talk politics
by mail it's like aiming ten or fifteen degrees away from where
the voice is coming from; let's save it for over beer. And DuBois,
too, whom I still see as an advocate of and apologist for slaveyy,
but then the Hungarian Negroes are on the other side of his double
standard. I'm sorry...politics, again.

These have been troubled months. That albatross I wear
on the inside's been squawking. Mostly, I hate the work I do for
a living, but this house I've bought has built a standard of
living under and around me I can't escape.

When do you get home? Before this script gets before the
cameras, I hope. Honest, I can't tell them what the inside of
a French jail looks like. Does it look like my air-conditioned
cell at the Research Institute of America? When I read EQUAL,
it _feels_ like it. Know a lawyer I can call?

Write soon.

Best,

March 2, 1958

The clipping I sent Baldwin and referred to in my letter was from *The New York Times* and must have referred to Baldwin's "authority" and "power." I did not preserve a copy of the clipping.

March 2, 1958

Dear Authority and Power,

Should you not be reading the New York Times, the enclosed clip will bear out my salutation. From today's paper...

When are you returning? Have to set myself some arbitrary deadline on finishing ANTRIM'S MONEY--writing it, not spending it-- and why not the date when a reader becomes available.

Fitelson told me about the Kazan deal. I will be holding my breath. I and mine (all 4) are prepared to live off handouts from you, despite the line.

Best,

March 3, 1958

After *Notes of a Native Son* was published I continued to provide Baldwin with editorial comments on manuscripts. Here he acknowledges such notes. In the last lines he is referring to my wife by her nickname and three of our sons, two of whom are pictured with Baldwin elsewhere in the book.

MacDowell Colony
PETERBOROUGH
N. H.

Dear Sol:

Bless you.

HARD at work, and practically
inhuman, socially speaking, therefore. Will
make use of your notes one of these days—yes,
they were very helpful—and hops to have
filled one of the folders by the time I
make my next descent into the maelstrom.
To you, and Sunnis, And Kevin, and Joff, and
Dana, my love.   Jim

July 30, 1958
Postmarked France

Baldwin was not quite thirty-four when he wrote this letter,
feeling old in Paris. The novel he was working on was probably
Another Country, which was published in 1962. I wasn't concerned about money.

Dear Sol :

Sorry to have been so precipitate, many things
happened at once. And I had to make a decision at once. So.
Here I am, in an apartment in the country which belongs to a
friend, working my ass off - on the novel - and also getting
some notion of where I am, and where I'm to go from here. I'll
be back on or about Labor Day.

I don't imagine that anything will be happening in
the city this summer which particularly requires my attention,
but if urgent professional matters come up, there's Helen Straus,
of course, and my address here is, as before, simply American
Express, Paris.

It's nice to be here in a way, in a somewhat different
way than ever before. I don't seem to know anybody here anymore,
except professionally. The generation now to be found on the cafe
terraces makes me feel rather old- and, of course, I'm here as a
tourist this time, which changes many things. The situation here,
for all that everyone says that Paris is exactly the same, is
simply grim. Everyone is waiting, nothing has been decided- as
regards,I mean, the problems facing this country - and the French
are tighter and harder than ever. The inter-racial climate, a phrase
I never expected to be using in relation to Paris, is very unpleasant
indeed; not on the surface; in the eyes, in tones of voice, in the
way that Frenchmen look at Algerians; and the way the Algerians
look back. I wouldn't like to be a Frenchman now, any more than I
would like to be a white man in the South.

Well. I stick to my house, to my typewriter, go out

shopping late every afternoon, watch the population of this small
town - which is also watching me - have a drink, come home, eat,
work some more, go to bed. Beautifully dull, beautifully exhausting.
No-one ever comes to see me, for I'm too far away for a casual visit.
I don't have any phone. Don't even drink very much, for I don't like
solitary drinking. Go to Paris tomorrow to pick up my mail. And I
hope that I can manage to keep this up throughout the summer. If I
do, I'll come home with a novel - which, at this moment, is going
quite well.

Getting on the plane, especially the way I did it, took
all the money I had. There was a little money owed me here, on which
I've been living;more should be coming through in a couple of weeks
and I'll send you your thirty dollars. I'm sorry to have made you
wait so long for it.

Of course, the thing which shook together all of my
indecisions into this decision was, at bottom, personal. Of course,
it involves Lucien, whom I have not yet seen, and it involves - well,
for the lack of a better word, let us say my freedom. But I cannot
talk about this yet, I will talk to you about it when I get back.

Give my love to Sunnie and the kids, and keep in touch
with me.

See you soon.

Love,

Jimmy

The second page of the letter that follows calls for a bit of
background. I had worked at the Research Institute of America,
superintending about ten publications directed to the chief ex-
ecutives of member firms. Out of a severe case of loyalty to my
boss, Leo Cherne, who was better known as the longtime head
of the International Rescue Committee and not known as the
longtime member of the Foreign Intelligence Advisory Board,
serving under six presidents of both parties, I felt I couldn't re-
sign from the institute on short notice, though I had firm plans
to start a new book club that would be launched in 1959 as the
Mid-Century Book Society. I decided to shift to a job in advertising, a field I believed I could easily leave on short notice.

My first duty at McCann-Erickson was to name a product.
I did that in the first hour of the first day. I was told to put my
result in my desk drawer for a week because they couldn't bill
the client for just an hour's work. My last job at McCann was
hastily writing a new book for a musical produced by McCann
called *Bad Day at 50 Rock* that was already in rehearsal and
scheduled to open at the Starlight Roof of the Waldorf shortly
and then tour to Chicago and Los Angeles. The show had a
problem. The set was built, the songs were fine, the actors
seemed to be doing well; it was just that the book (the story)

Sol Stein and James Baldwin (back row) at the MacDowell
Colony in 1954, the years they put together *Notes of a Native
Son*. Some of the other artists in residence were composer
Irving Fine, who was chairman of the School of Creative Arts
at Brandeis; painter Gregory Prestopino, whose work hangs in
eighteen museums, including the Museum of Modern Art; com-
posers Otto Luening, Louise Talma, and Vladimir Ussachevsky;
Pulitzer Prize–winning poet Peter Viereck; and painter Milton
Avery. Avery's work now hangs in the Metropolitan Museum of
Art, the National Gallery of Art, and sixty-six other museums.
The photograph on the back jacket of this book is from this
group photograph. PHOTOGRAPH COURTESY OF THE ESTATE OF BERNICE PERRY.

Two of the earliest known photos of James Baldwin, taken by
Sol Stein, and photos of Stein taken by Baldwin with the same
camera on the same day. Baldwin, is standing near the apartment house on West 177th Street in Manhattan, where the
Stein family lived when Sol went into active service on March
1, 1945. Seen in the background is the George Washington
bridge when it had just a single level. The apartment house was
subsequently razed when a second level was added to the
bridge. These snapshots were probably taken in late December
1946, when Sol Stein returned from Germany but had not yet
been demobilized. PHOTOGRAPHS COURTESY OF SOL STEIN.

Baldwin in the living room of Sol Stein's first house, located in Forest Hills, New York. PHOTOGRAPH COURTESY OF SOL STEIN.

Baldwin pinching the cheek of Kevin Stein, the oldest of Stein's six sons. It was probably taken a few years after the publication of *Notes of a Native Son*. Baldwin had a lot of practice with young children at home and with Stein's children as well.

PHOTOGRAPH COURTESY OF SOL STEIN.

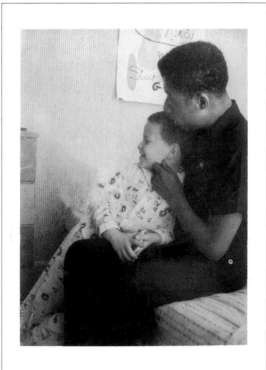

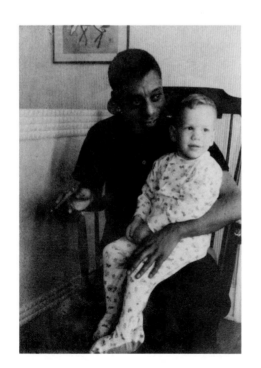

James Baldwin holding Leland Dana Stein, whose birth was noticed in one of Stein's letters and in Baldwin's response to Leland's name. PHOTOGRAPH COURTESY OF SOL STEIN.

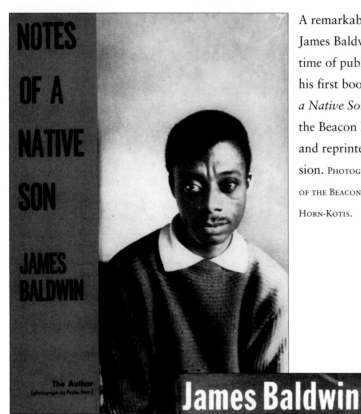

NOTES OF A NATIVE SON

JAMES BALDWIN

The Author
[photograph by Paula Horn]

James Baldwin

NOBODY KNOWS MY NAME

MORE NOTES OF A NATIVE SON

A remarkable photo of James Baldwin at the time of publication of his first book, *Notes of a Native Son,* published by the Beacon Press, Boston, and reprinted with permission. PHOTOGRAPH COURTESY OF THE BEACON PRESS AND PAULA HORN-KOTIS.

The jacket of the original edition of James Baldwin's second book of essays, *Nobody Knows My Name.* USED BY PERMISSION OF DOUBLEDAY, A DIVISION OF RANDOM HOUSE, INC.

for my brothers,
George, Wilmer,
and
David

for Sol :—
In honor of the splendidly
disputed passage.
love,
God help us.
jimmy

To Sol—
With affection, and esteem
and to a long, long association.
jimmy
Aug., 1954

The original of this photograph was presented to Stein by the photographer, Joseph A. Maynard IV. Stein had just finished a long day at the Schomburg Center for Research in Black Culture on Malcolm X Boulevard in Manhattan, where a documentary called *Prelude to a Movement: Black Paris and the Struggle for Freedom* was being filmed and in which Stein spoke about Baldwin. After more than eight intensive hours of filming, Stein headed for the nearest subway station, which was empty except for one person who was reading a copy of *Notes of a Native Son* while waiting. Stein initiated a conversation with Maynard, a professional photographer, who turned out to have photographed Baldwin in 1976 in New York City. Some months later Maynard visited with Stein and presented him with the framed original of this photograph, which Stein liked especially because it shows Baldwin in repose, in contrast to most of the published photographs.

COURTESY OF JOSEPH A. MAYNARD IV.

didn't work. Frank Armstrong, the producer, and Samuel (Biff) Liff, the director, were worried because McCann had already invited the head honchos of their best prospective clients to the black-tie opening. Someone alerted Armstrong to the fact that I'd had two plays produced. I was immediately set to writing a new book for the musical, funneling pages to the actors for memorization. I was the only one at the opening not in black tie because I had still been writing lines that afternoon. I viewed the play from behind a set of lights up in the balcony. The play was a hit. Afterward, my boss, overflowing with relief and congratulations, said I could write my own ticket at McCann. I reported sadly that I was coming to see him Monday morning to give notice because I was all set to launch the new book club, which took me a step closer to my long career as an editor and publisher.

August 9, 1958

Dear Jimmy,

I'm glad you wrote.

You were a preacher once. Whenever I sit down tox write to
you, or sometimes when we just talk without time enough to get
under anything, I get in a preachy mood, and I'm beginning to hate
it now. I think it comes from accepting the surfaces of the ways
we live: you an irresponsibly non-bohemian-bohemian anti-bengal
free lance charging into your typewriter or your conscience every
day; and me, a family-owing, house-owning, Madisonavenuer-of-sorts,
with a wristalarm to remind me of time and when to run to the analyst,
steeling himself against adaptations in the hope (dread) of finding
out whether I'm a writer or no writer. The grass is greener. Money
and time are real. A writer is someone who writes well, and the whole
kit-and-kaboodle of cliches don't really deserve either of our
postures, not when talking or writing to each ather, anyway. We're
both running, and the business of life is independence not running.
I think one needs a crushing conscience so one can love people worth
loving when they're divorced from their pack, and to have the guts
to be alone (which is where writing and politics are made). The people
I admire who are safely dead in history learned to run, for their
independence, to their studies.

I think now, late, we're both trying to do that. What makes
me feel guilty about my way are social cliches about people who
function in the real world, only that world, cliche again, is no
more real than the security and acceptability it's supposed to provide.
And what brings out the discomfort when I face you is the condescension
you have been dropping bit by bit since we picked up being friends
again and I have the restlessness and resentment of an NAACP'er
about speeding up what takes time. I want to be a white man, which
means seen out of my context, which seems to stand like walls around
me whenever you go over the border to Paris or somewhere or come
to our appointments late enough for me to feel like Murphy cooling
his heels outside Nasser's office (no other simile applied implied
than the feeling of being able to offend, however guiltily, however
purposeful).

Let's have that talk about freedom when you get back.

What got me off on this as much as anything is your mention
of the Algerians. You'd hate to be a Frenchman now. I'd hate
to be an Algerian now, too. Our job is to see. Jacobinism as well
as Imperial Pride, that is. The play is seeing both, the souring of
a virtue. Radicals and reactionaries drink the sour stuff, go blind.
Liberals taste a little at a time, immunizing themselves against
the dangers of either, they think, but drinking sour stuff just the
same. The writer's trade is to watch them all so that one can make
predictions about human behavior; that's when the imagination can
work well, when what hasn't happened, happens. Let's talk about
the way I see black and you see white. That's the conversation I
want to learn from.

let's not talk
about Algerians.

Now to prose (a poet's conceit). On the 15th I leave the
Research Institute. On September 2nd, I after a brief vacation,
I join a subsidiary of McCann-Erickson, the no. 2 advertising
agency, where I will be doing everything but advertising. I have
set up, formally, a lot of no tresspassing signs; let's see how
well they're observed. I can be detached about it because I have
signed contracts in my pocket for February 1, when I expect to
move into a place to stay. Less money, but only half-time work.
I will superintend the editorial end of a conglomeration of
things: The Readers Subscription (the Trilling, Barzun, Auden
book club), The Theatre Library, Playbill, Souvenir Books (e.g.
the Brussels World Fair program, the good one), The Ambassador, *several interesting magazines*
and the Fielding Press, a publishing firm intended to give
authors the editors they want, whatever their affiliation, and
a chance to make out financially on books of quality. No options;
a continuing voluntary arrangement with the men whose books are
designed to last. I'll have an equity in the firm, full veto
power over nonsense, and a first-rate staff of grown-up people.

Rushed desperately to you with the full revision of "Antrim's
Money" just a day or two too late. It'll keep till September.
We how know what Ella does on her day off, and the result is, one
reader thought she was the finest person in the play. Sam is still
all there, and Margo and the boy have come up a bit--but both these
still need work.

If you want to, come February we could work out a Guggenheim-plus
type of arrangement, where you'd get what you need a month to write
short and long but what you want to--provided it can be talked out
and worked out in a way which will provide rather than restrict
your sense of freedom. That's what the job is supposed to do for
me, and what I can do with the job ought to be able to do the same
for some others.

We all love you and look to your homecoming, soon.

P.S. Looking back, I dislike this let ter for the way it says
intricate things too quickly. Please fill in the interstices,
with affection at least. I think I depend on our friendship more
than on any other. You are the only friend with whom I feel
comfortable about all three: heart, head, and writing.

Erasing History

A Prefatory Word About the Story "Dark Runner"
and the Television Play *Equal in Paris*

The meaning of words change with time. In the story and play that follow, written in 1957, the protagonist is referred to as a "twenty-five-year-old boy," language one would never use today. Our intention at the time was to describe a fictional character called Billy Ade, based on a traumatic event in Baldwin's life when he was twenty-five. It was first reported in Baldwin's essay, "Equal in Paris," which appeared in *Notes of a Native Son.* Our intention was to have the character resemble Jimmy as he looked on the jacket of the original edition of *Notes,* dressed in a too-big sweater and with a white dicky collar setting off his then boyish face. Though we were far from innocent at twenty-five, we still thought of ourselves as boys, for indeed we were when we met, and some of that stuck. As reported elsewhere, at Baldwin's six-tieth birthday celebration, he introduced me around as his "high-school buddy" and in a new preface to the 1984 edition of *Notes,* he began, "It was Sol Stein, high-school buddy . . . ," giving pri-macy to how we still saw ourselves. The term "boy" applied to an adult had for us an innocent connotation, and it would be un-like either of us to erase history for the sake of political correct-ness. Both the story and the play that follow are as they were at the time we wrote them half a century ago.

What in heaven's name were Baldwin and Stein thinking about when they collaborated on a play for the new and reductive medium of television, which was not receptive to the nuance and character that are welcome in fiction, nonfiction and, at times, in the legitimate theater?

The answer is money. Neither Baldwin nor I had earned anything that could be called a living from our writings up to that time. To declare the actual amounts we'd each earned from books and theater would be embarrassing on the same page as our responsibilities. I had three young Steinlings, and Baldwin felt responsibility to help his widowed mother out with his eight younger siblings. Television money was real, and half of it was paid in advance. One might add an enticement that Baldwin and I never spoke about. Television, though reductive, had this huge audience out there, and so despite our prior more complex work we seized on the opportunity to do a script for the Theater Guild. It asked us to write a synopsis. Graham Greene, in the second volume of his autobiography, said, "For me it is impossible to write a film play without first writing a story. A film depends on more than plot; it depends on a certain measure of characterization, on mood and atmosphere, and these seem impossible to capture for the first time in the dull shorthand of a conventional treatment." Like Greene, neither Baldwin nor I liked the idea of writing a synopsis so we wrote a story and called it a synopsis. The title we gave the story was "Dark Runner." For the television play that appears in the appendix to this book, we used the same title as Baldwin's nonfiction essay "Equal in Paris," from which both the story and the play are derived.

Our comeuppance for the trip into the world of television came when, in the end, the Theater Guild wanted us to change the black protagonist to white, which, given the story, made no sense. I'd wager the grafted love story and the sentimental ending would be dealt with swiftly if the old friends could collaborate for a few hours more today when television is more receptive to a protagonist being both gay and black.

S.S., December 2003

"Dark Runner"

by Sol Stein and James Baldwin

At first, no title or credits.

Just the camera discovering in the darkness of the screen a marvelous face, a tall, thin Negro boy of twenty-five with large large eyes. Billy Ade wears a sweater much too big, someone else's perhaps. A white dickey collar sets off his face, a sad black moon. The camera circles around him as if we were looking at a piece of sculpture, which, in a way, we are.

In the background, a pulse of sound, perhaps the echo of a drum in a faraway jungle. Billy lights the butt of a cigarette which has been smoked before, and speaks:

"This story starts in Africa maybe, three hundred years ago. Or maybe in Harlem, the hour I was born, slapped and screaming. Or it could have begun when my father, tall and black as an African tribal chieftain, started reading the King James Bible aloud to me."

The somber lights surrounding Billy flicker with the shadows of violence. His face conveys the fear of long ago.

"My father told me God was a God of justice and vengeance, and I was frightened. He told me God was a God of mercy, and I was confused. In my father's face, King James fused with the King of the Jungle, and I didn't know who I was, or where I belonged, and so . . ." The camera has now circled around to the rear of Billy. "I turned my back and started to run."

The drum-beat blends into the sound of a pair of hurrying feet, then the blast of a police whistle, as the camera follows the fast-moving feet, the title rolls across the screen: DARK RUNNER. As the credits come on, the running feet slow down, the distant drum blends with the sound of a single string plucked on a bass fiddle, the rhythm loosens, falls apart, become[s] the beat of jazz. As the last credits distort and fade, we find ourselves at a party, legs dancing, mouths laughing, whispering, the cleft of a bosom, lips at an ear, intimations of sexuality, drinking drunk, bursts of hysterical laughter, and through it all, that beat: jazz, Greenwich Village, New York.

Cut to a black finger poking the doorbell. Then, inside the party-loud apartment, the camera follows the Negro maid out of the kitchen to the door. Billy Ade stands there, looking at once lost and proud, holding a bulky parcel. The maid supposes he is a delivery boy and asks, "That package for Mr. Ravedon?" She reaches for the package, which Billy, defensively, holds back. He says nothing. And the maid, embarrassed, quickly says: "Well, come on in." He nods and enters, immediately greeted by the crowd of celebrants, those who know him and those who don't, handed a drink and enveloped by white faces chattering in frantic cordiality. He is the only Negro there.

The hostess, a giddy, rich, white woman by the name of Watson[,] takes Billy in tow and steers him to the guest of honor, a well-dressed man of 40. "This is Maurice Portnoy," she bubbles, "just the brightest lawyer in New York, and Billy here, Billy

Ade, is just the brightest young writer in the country today, just won that Rockefeller or Ford or whatever-the-name-is fellowship. . . ." and she is off to greet another guest, leaving Maurice and Billy in a noise-surrounded cocoon of embarrassment.

"Second brightest," says Maurice. "Me too," says Billy, and they both smile and shake hands. "What's the occasion?" asks Billy, waving at the celebrants. Maurice answers, "I'm off to Paris for a year, nice assignment from my firm, and I guess there wasn't any other excuse for a party this week, so here we are."

"Madhouse," says Billy, shouting to make himself heard, aware that Maurice's eyes are on the parcel Billy is clutching. "Manuscript," he explains. "Book. Novel. Not quite finished. Don't dare leave it home. I've got something like a hundred brothers and sisters around the house, most of them young enough to draw on anything they get their hands on."

"How do you get your work done?" asks Maurice.

"A miracle," answers Billy.

"Why don't you come to Paris. Great place for writers, I hear."

"For lawyers?"

"Writers!"

"Don't have a firm to send me," laughs Billy.

"How about that fellowship?"

But Mrs. Watson is upon them again, introducing a newcomer, and Maurice is barely able to get a card to Billy on which he scribbles a Paris address "in case you come."

Mrs. Watson introduces the newcomer standing helplessly beside her. As camouflage for his shyness, he wears a beard. He calls himself Square. He has left his wealthy parents in Princeton and fled with his clarinet to the Village.

Billy, who is stranger-shy, tries, out of politeness, to say a word or two about jazz, and says it so well we immediately see Square's response as that of admiration. But Mrs. Watson is still twittering about, hostessy. To Billy she says, "I think it's wonderful you received that fellowship instead of somebody with . . . well, you know . . . all those advantages."

"Which advantages?" says Billy.

"I guess she means me," says Square, "my folks are rich like Mrs. Watson here," and the boys laugh together, as Mrs. Watson flees to welcome other guests.

One blue-jeaned guest is quite far gone in drink and browsing for trouble. His name is Dirk, a painter of sorts, one of whose mad pictures adorns Mrs. Watson's walls. He's having difficulty finding someone to bait until he lights on Square because of his beard. Billy is amused by Dirk's foolishness at first, but then becomes apprehensive as Dirk announces that he uses neither a brush nor a palette-knife for his violent paintings, but a switchblade knife, which he suddenly flourishes in the direction of Square's beard.

Billy is forced to intervene by taking Dirk's knife out of his hands with calm deliberateness. He closes the blade. Others at the party are now watching them. Dirk, threatened by shame, snatches back his knife, flips the blade open, and with one violent movement hurls it into the carpeted floor, hushing the crowd into silence.

"Mrs. Watson," says Billy, "you have a guest with bad manners."

Exactly what Dirk calls Billy is drowned in the noise of comment, but everyone knows what was intended.

Billy controls his rage only long enough to pluck the knife from the carpet, again closes it, and hands it to Mrs. Watson, who, with studied politeness, takes Dirk to the door, suggesting he call for the knife the next day when he is "feeling better" and [lets] his "marvelously passionate nature" [loose] on some of those "indescribably beautiful paintings." At this there is general laughter, except from Billy and Square. Square alone sees how upset Billy is.

"Don't pay any attention what he said," says Square, "he's loaded."

"I've had a lot of practice not paying attention," says Billy bitterly. "I'm getting the hell out of here."

Square follows him, saying he wants to leave the noise behind also, and suggests Billy join him in a night-cap at his place nearby. "I'm e-ternally grateful to you," says Square in one of his obviously favorite phrases, as they go out.

In the street, we follow them through the strange juxtapositions of Greenwich Village: the modern buildings for the wealthy, like the one they have just left, and around the corner, the aging tenements of the Italians, the artists, the derelicts, the young runaways, the poor, and the bohemians at every stage of sanity.

We dissolve to Square's room, decrepit because he is fleeing a rich home, just as he wears a beard to cover his handsome face and odd clothes because his parents brought him up in Rogers Peet suits. It is in Square's room that these things become clear to us, and we see the beginning of a bond between two lonely people.

Square suddenly decides to call his parents' home in Princeton, although Billy objects that it is too late to phone. Square insists, and from his end of the conversation we gather that he has indeed awakened his parents, disturbed them, has to assure them that it's not an emergency, that he is only inquiring if he may bring a friend home to dinner the following night. We are aware of his conspicuous failure to mention Billy's color. Square seems to enjoy the anticipation of the shock and discomfort awaiting his parents when he brings Billy home.

The scene in the home of Square's parents is a mixture of comedy and pain. After the first shock, Square's parents try to make Billy "comfortable," refer to the "liberal" college community around them, the seven or eight Negroes at Princeton this year, and so on, making it plain that they have never met a Negro on such a footing before in their lives. Square realizes that he has not only made his parents uncomfortable, but has created a terrible situation for Billy, also. We see the war of pride in the way Square's father, after dinner, offers both boys cigars, in the troubled expression Billy has as he waits to have his cigar lighted,

and in the difficulty of Square's father as he
lights his cigar. The discomfort is too much for
all of them, and as soon as it is decently possible, the boys leave.

We hear the tense, jazz background again as the
boys walk the streets of Princeton, pass an all-
night diner, and, at Square's suggestion, go in for
a cup of coffee.

The place is decorated in flamboyant bad taste,
one wall a garish mirror. Square and Billy seat
themselves. The fat counterman shuffles up to
them.

"Cup of coffee," says Square.

"Two," says Billy.

"Don't serve any . . . ," says the counterman,
making it apparent that Billy is not welcome. The
boys refuse to take the hint.

"Any more what?" says Billy.

"Any more tonight," says the counterman.

To make his point clear, the counterman brings
over a single cup of coffee and puts it in front of
Square.

The fury of the jazz tempo mounts. Billy, hurt
by his encounters with Dirk and then Square's parents, now faces the counterman in anger. Square at-
tempts to calm Billy as the fat counterman tries to
outstare Billy's hatred with his own. "Now get out
of here," he says, coming around the end of the
counter. The jazz tempo races madly as Billy, with
one furious motion, lifts Square's coffee cup and
hurls it at the counterman. It misses, strikes the
mirrored wall, which shatters as all the customers
rise to their feet.

"Run," says Square.

Billy is as frightened as everyone else at what he has done.

Billy brushes past those who try to stop him as he makes his way to the street, clutching his manuscript. Square, breathless beside him, says: "What did you do that for?"

"What did you take me in there for?" Billy shouts back.

"You could have killed him!"

"I wanted to!"

The shouts of the counterman are answered by the blast of a police whistle a block distant.

Again Square says: "Run!" Billy runs like hell, with Square pacing beside him. "Duck in there," says Square as they pass an alleyway. Billy does so, and Square continues straight ahead, to decoy the policeman away.

Cut to Billy, blocks away and still running. Suddenly out of the shadows steps a cop with a nightstick and Billy sees him too late to keep from running smack into him.

"Where you running to, boy?" says the cop.

"Home," says Billy in fright.

"Why so fast, boy?" says the cop, taking him by an arm.

Billy tries to control his breathlessness. "Please let me go. If I don't catch that train, my mother'll give me hell. I'm supposed to be back in New York already."

"What's that you got under your arm?"

"This? It's a book."

"That doesn't look like a book." He drags Billy over closer to the street light. "You steal something, kid?"

"No," says Billy. "It's a book, honest. It's a manuscript."

"A what?"

"A thing I'm writing."

"Don't you lie to me, boy!" The policeman takes the package from Billy, riffles suspiciously through the papers, finally bursts out laughing as he hands the package back to Billy and sends him on his way. This laughter rings in Billy's ears as we fade out.

Fade in on a Harlem tenement, Billy mounting the stoop, then up six dreary, littered flights of stairs. He opens the door, and surveys his home in the darkness. The camera goes with him through the rooms, which seem to be filled to overflowing with sleeping children (Billy's younger brothers and sisters). We hear the sound of his mother's voice from the bedroom.

"That you, Billy?"

On her elbow, her words still cottony with sleep, she admonishes him for being so late, endangering his health, going to parties, and so on, until she realizes he is near tears, at which she becomes wide awake, comforting, asking, consoling in words that ring his private world but dare not enter.

He tells her he nearly killed a man, that his anger has burst, that trying "not to pay attention" no longer works. It is as if all of his life pointed toward the flinging of that coffee cup. He has made up his mind, he tells her, he is going to take his fellowship money and get to Europe, anywhere, but away. His mother cautions that he cannot escape from himself, that he takes himself with him wherever he goes. Billy counters by saying, there are places where people will treat him "like everybody else." His mother says he must learn to wrestle with it here, but says he should go if he feels he must.

The youngest child, a little girl, gets out of bed for comfort and a glass of water, and Billy tenderly puts her back to bed, gives her the water, and sings her softly to sleep again. He looks up to see his mother watching him with the child in his arms, and he feels the weight of his fatherless home resting on him.

"I *have* to go away, Mom," he says.

"I know," she says quietly.

We cut to his face, then hers, then his again, as their eyes fill with tears long prepared for. Fade out.

We fade in from a high place, to the sound of a jazz trumpet. The music has changed its character from American to French. We are looking down from the Arch of Triumph onto the black speck of a boy standing far beneath it, his manuscript under his arm. Paris.

We take Billy through a montage of days and weeks, cutting back and forth between work and loneliness. His hurried pecks at the typewriter, the wasted pages balled into the wastebasket in anger, the momentary smile when a paragraph succeeds. And between these images, the streets and sounds of Paris, Billy buying cigarettes, asking directions, which, when given, he clearly fails to understand. Or sitting at a café terrace, watching the immense friendliness of Paris, and yet not sharing in it because he has taken his shyness with him. Once, we see Billy, walking alone on a side street, pass a Senegalese soldier. After they pass, they stop and turn back and look at each other, the length of street between them, and then they move on to their separate loneliness.

Billy in his room, writing to his mother, then working at the typewriter, working, working, and suddenly, again on the street, the world of New York comes crashing back to him, unbelievingly, but there he is: Square. They clap each other on the back, enthuse, and romp off to a jazz club, where Square, newly arrived in Paris, has found his place. He tells Billy he is playing there with a jazz group and having the time of his life. "I finally found a good use for my parents," he says. "I took some of their money and came here."

At the club, it is apparent that Square has found people who accept him. Billy catches sight of one of the performers at the club, a dancer, a beautiful, young Negro girl. Billy asks Square who she is, but Square is intent on other things.

"I'm staying at a place called the Hotel de Deux Arbres, two trees but not a tree in sight. A real hellhole. The owner's a thief and his wife's a nymphomaniac, and neither of them will leave me alone. Where are you living?"

"At the Grand Hotel du Bac," says Billy. "It's a joint."

"Good, good," says Square, "they got a room for me?"

Billy still has the dancer in his line of vision, but knows it is a lost cause. He takes Square to his hotel.

Dissolve to the hallway of the Hotel du Bac, just outside Billy's room. "That's your room down the hall," says Billy, "fourteen."

"E-ternally grateful," responds Square, lugging his suitcases down the hall. Billy enters his own room. The bed is unmade, the linen rumpled. He drops down on the bed, closes his eyes, resting from Square's enthusiasm. A knock on the door, and before Billy can answer, it swings open. Square, quick[ly] becoming an e-ternal nuisance, exclaims his room is fabulous, sees Billy's crumpled bed, asks when they change the linen.

"They never change it," says Billy. "At least if they *made* the beds, I wouldn't have to look at it."

Square darts out, comes back with a clean, folded sheet . . . with his compliments. He whips off the sheet on Billy's bed and remakes it. Square's personality has blossomed in Paris, and he has taken to wisecracking, something new to him. "Thrown any coffee cups lately?" he asks. Billy, annoyed, pleads tiredness, and finally gets Square out of the room.

Later, Billy is just finishing off a letter to his baby sister and goes off to mail it—and to see if there's any mail from home at the American Express. There, among the patrons, he catches a fleeting glimpse of the same young dancer he saw at Square's club. He tries, in his shy way, to introduce himself to her, something very difficult for him in any case, and she quickly and efficiently brushes him off.

Back at his room, Billy is disconsolate, tells Square of the incident with the girl. Square has an idea. He'll order a table after the show at the jazz club that night, invite a number of guests, asks if there's anyone Billy would like to invite. Billy suggests Maurice Portnoy. Square says fine. Then gingerly, Billy suggests the dancer. With a wink, Square says he'll try.

At the jazz club that evening, Billy finds a number of Square's new friends, French jazz musicians; Maurice, whom Billy is glad to see; and a tourist, an American Negro publisher, who, Billy suspects, was invited by Square to make Billy feel "more comfortable." If so, he has succeeded only in putting Billy further on edge, especially because the publisher is obviously an ass, as his conversation soon establishes. When Square finishes his musical chores, he joins them at the table. The next act is the young Negro dancer, and Billy's excitement grows. Her dancing is youthful, good, and frankly sexual. We cut rapidly to face after face in the audience, then Billy's, transfixed.

After the girl's number, she comes down to join them at their table. Billy's heart leaps when Square introduces her all around ("This is Siddy St. Clare") and seats her next to Billy.

She has a sweet smile she cannot hide, hard as she tries. Billy searches for a way to begin talking to her.

"You must be an American," he says.

She laughs. "How in the world did you ever guess that!"

To cover his embarrassment, Billy says, "I saw you at American Express."

"Oh you were the one," she says, and is again

amused at Billy's expense. But she notices his discomfort and tries to assuage it.

"I suppose you're an American, too?" she says.

"I'm a Senegalese," says Billy.

"Oh I'll bet!"

"My father's a headhunter."

"Oh I'll bet!"

"You don't believe me?" says Billy, beginning to
spark.

"Senegalese have a lovely lilt in their voices.
They speak beautifully. You sound like you're from
New Jersey."

"You win," says Billy, and she smiles in a way
that lets Billy know that they are friends.

Billy admires her dancing, and she asks him what
he does. He tells her about the novel. "I started
out writing poems, songs, unsaleable things. In a
high school I got a letter from Mayor LaGuardia for
winning a poetry prize and it went to my head. I
haven't stopped writing since. How long have you
been dancing?"

"Always," says Siddy. "I did handstands at three,
a tap-dance in my first-grade musical, heard applause, and have been sunk ever since. My father, he
says, 'Crazy girl, what do you want to dance for,
can't you walk like everybody else does?' " We learn
that she is from Atlanta, that it cost her father a
terrible price to become a doctor there, raise her
in an environment hostile to her race and in a Negro
community even more hostile to her dancing, making
fun of her until she fled to New York and then to
Paris with a troupe. "Did your father let you be a
writer?" she asks.

"Heavens, no," says Billy. "My father, he's dead

now, he wanted me to become a preacher, a bellering, yellering, praise-the-Lord preacher. When I was fourteen I became a preacher. When I was seventeen I stopped. The world's been going to blazes ever since."

They both laugh. Billy continues, "The world is nothing less than a conspiracy against the cultivation of my talent. Especially since I don't make any money at it. Which is a pity."

"Maybe the novel'll be published," says Siddy.

He answers, "It'll be finished in a week."

"I hope it's a good week," says Siddy.

"It's bound to be. Now."

He tries to put his hand on hers, but she avoids it gracefully.

"What do you really want to be?" he asks.

"Just the world's greatest dancer. And you?"

"An honest man. And a good writer."

The colored publisher has been trying to edge into the conversation, boorishly. He clashes with Billy, which merely establishes a greater rapport between him and the girl. Billy is angry. Seeing this, Square says, "Maybe they'd better cover up the mirror over there!" which infuriates Billy. He is anxious not to explain the meaning of the remark, especially in front of the girl. He tries to get her to take a walk with him, but she suggests it's late and they make a date for the next day.

Their walk through Paris the next day is an event of discovery. The pretext: she is looking for a new pair of dancing shoes she saw somewhere along the Champs-Elysées. They pass the places previously seen in Billy's loneliness. They browse at a bookstore. They see a Renault in a showroom window

and joke about taking it back home, driving around
Atlanta with the top open, Billy wearing a turban,
"a Sheik," he says, "a chic Sheik," and they warm
together in their laughter.

But soon she must run for her performance, and
she breaks the news, with sadness, that the troupe
she came over with leaves the next afternoon for
Rome.

Billy says he'll pick her up after the show that
night. He does, brings flowers, but Siddy is sur-
rounded by members of her troupe who have come to
see her farewell performance at the jazz club, and
they all go off to the hotel where the troupe and
Siddy are staying, and there are just too many people around. They decide to meet the next morning
and to spend the day together, from an early breakfast right through to train time.

"You won't get your novel finished that way,"
she says, and Billy responds by damning the novel
and kissing her.

To avoid the people in her troupe at the hotel,
she says she'll pick him up at his place. And for
the night, he turns over to her his most precious
possession, the manuscript of his novel. We fade
out on an image of Siddy in her room, reading the
precious pages.

All joy, Billy skips back to his hotel, antici-
pating the next day, which Siddy will spend with him.

He knocks at Square's door, enters, is surprised
to see two French policemen examining Square's
identification papers. Billy and Square, both puzzled and a bit frightened, try to laugh things off
with the policemen. But the police insist on see-

ing Billy's room, which, he argues, isn't very presentable. When the policemen enter Billy's room, one goes instantly to the bed, lifts the pillow, and at once Billy realizes what has happened. On the new bedsheet the words "Hotel des Deux Arbres" stand out large and clear—the hotel at which Square had been staying.

Billy and Square are hauled off the police station, assuring themselves, though not very successfully, that nothing serious is involved. They are forbidden to contact their embassy or even a lawyer.

They are in the hands of French custom. It turns out that the "man in authority" at the police station isn't there and the boys are locked up for the night in a cell. Billy is suddenly frantic, remembering his date with Siddy, who is coming to his hotel in the morning and who is leaving that afternoon for Rome. "I won't know where to find her," he begs the police. "Please let me call somebody." The policeman makes it clear he's to get no special treatment, even if he is an American. Here they are to be treated like any Frenchman. The door of the "chicken coop" slams shut.

We fade in the following morning. Billy and Square, sleep still in their eyes, handcuffed, are taken out into the gray drizzle of a French morning and shoved into a black police car. Dissolve to the car pulling up in front of what looks like a decrepit fortress.

"What is this?" asks Billy.

"The prison," he is told.

"But we haven't even . . . but you can't take us

here, we're not . . ." His protests are drowned in the rain.

Cut to Siddy, also in the rain, manuscript in hand, arriving at the Hotel du Bac, her eyes still filled with sleep. She asks for Billy. The hotel owner says that Billy is gone. (He is ashamed to say that a guest has been taken off to jail.)

"Where did he go?" she asks.

"Who knows?" says the hotel owner, shrugging his shoulders. "Perhaps to America."

"No message."

Cut to a room of the prison where Square is being photographed and Billy is being fingerprinted. Billy's answers to the policeman's questions are sarcastic and bitter. He is photographed front view, side view. As the light flashes on his frightened face for the second picture, we cut to Siddy, still without breakfast, searching for Billy on this, her last day in Paris. She goes to the jazz club where they met, but it is closed, of course, at that hour of the morning.

Cut back to Billy and Square being locked up in a cell which already has three occupants: a seedy Arab peanut vendor, a youngster of 16, and a hoodlum who sits picking at his decayed teeth with a metal toothpick.

The jailer trundles in three garbage cans on wheels, the first with bread, the second coffee, the third a thick liquid, a kind of cousin to soup. There is some nervous by-play during the boys' first prison meal. In the middle of it, the two policemen come in for Billy and Square. As they lead the boys away, the other prisoners quickly pounce on the food Billy and Square have left behind.

The boys are taken to the interrogation room, where a man-in-authority is now behind the desk. A girl at a typewriter records everything. The boys are confronted by their accuser, the owner of the Hotel des Deux Arbres. Square is named as the thief, Billy as the receiver of stolen goods. The boys, unfamiliar with French ways and law, resist signing the transcript of the interrogation which the girl has typed. Billy, anxious to get out in time to meet Siddy, asks: "If I sign will it get us out faster?" The man in authority says: "Everything is always faster when one cooperates." Billy signs. Square signs. The boys are taken out a door as the camera rests on the seal over the door which proclaims "Liberté, Egalité, Fraternité."

Cut to Siddy, wandering the streets, echoing the loneliness of Billy's wanderings earlier, before he had met her. She is getting desperate. And everywhere she goes, Billy's manuscript is under her arm.

Cut back to the jail, where Billy and Square are going through the ignominy of having their shoelaces and belts taken away from them. They continue their private quarrel in a scene which ends with their awkwardly trying to come to blows while keeping their laceless and beltless clothes in place.

When the policeman takes them back into their cell, he angrily takes away the hoodlum's metal toothpick. As soon as the policeman leaves, however, the hoodlum scrambles to a crack in the wall where he had hidden another toothpick and shows it off to his fellow prisoners with enormous satisfaction.

The Arab is delousing his jacket. The 16-year-old picks his nose as if that is where his future lies.

The prisoners tease the newcomers about the "terrors" of French jails, tell a story about a man who was taken out of his cell, put on the wrong line, and guillotined in error.

Square joins the others in laughter at this, enraging Billy. He whirls around to face Square's grinning face. "What are you laughing at, goat beard? I've been in the wrong line, I know what it feels like when nothing, you've done nothing and you're in the wrong line. Like now. That's what I ran away from and wham! I'm right back where I started, just because you're a punk who steals things for kicks."

Square is stung. The other prisoners egg them on.

Square says, "You missed a date with a broad, one date, one broad, and you yell your head off. What would you be doing if you weren't in jail, smooching with the broad or writing that novel nobody wants to read???"

Billy tries defending his novel, the manuscript he would never let go and which is now—where?—and Square barks back, "Your novel, your so-what novel! I never met such a self-centered, whining, self-pitying guy in all my life! Don't you ever think of anybody except yourself?"

And Billy says, "Me? You see what I got all over me, this black? That's right, stare at it! I came here because I didn't want everybody to stare when they saw it. I didn't want people to look at me, I wanted them to forget me, and what do you do? You, you grow a beard so everybody'll notice you. They don't notice your clarinet-playing, but they'll

notice you all right when you parade around looking like a goat!"

And soon they are grappling, with the other
prisoners watching them with relish, and Square
saying, ". . . did you ever stop to think why I
grew a beard, why I needed the camouflage, that
maybe I needed it like you'd like to pick a color
that wasn't black? I can't pat my misery on the
back because I'm not white. When you ran away from
home, what were you running from, guys like yourself who cry about their own warts and laugh at
everybody else's?"

The policemen return. They handcuff Billy,
Square, and the 16-year-old, and take them to a police wagon, where each is shoved into a narrow cubicle just large enough for a man. So isolated, we
hear Billy say to the unseen Square, "I'm sorry."
The whispered response: "It's okay, kid." We see
the exhaust of the wagon as it roars off.

Cut to Siddy at her hotel, asking if there's a
message from Billy. She is clearly at her wit's
end. She sees a member of her troupe, learns they
are all packing already.

"Packing?" she says, "I haven't had breakfast
yet."

Cut back to the police wagon arriving at its
destination. The boys are taken before a judge in
a ramshackle courtroom. The 16-year-old is thrust
before the high bench first. The boy, defiant,
spits on the floor, is given six months for stealing a sweater. He is forcibly taken away, hurling
hatred with his eyes and voice.

Billy and Square are brought before the stern
judge.

The Judge asks, "These two, they are together?"

Policeman: "Yes, your honor. This one stole, this one received."

The Judge: "It says here they are Americans. Where is the interpreter?"

"Interpreter?"

"Idiots, there must be an interpreter for Americans. Take them back."

Billy says: "No! I don't need an interpreter. I live in Paris."

Judge: "This is your home?"

Billy: "I am living here."

Judge: "And stealing here?"

Billy: "I didn't steal."

Judge: "Boys should stay at home. The law says you must have an interpreter. Tomorrow is Christmas. You will be brought back after Christmas . . . with an interpreter. Take them away."

Cut to Siddy, who has returned to the Hotel du Bac. She asks if Billy has come back. The answer, of course, is no. Then she asks for Square, learns he, too, is gone. In a panic, she goes to American Express, to leave a message for Billy. We see her trying to write something, not knowing what to say, crossing things out, and holding back tears.

Cut to the boys being taken back to their cell. The Arab is wrapping some things in a handkerchief, preparing to leave. His term is over. The hoodlum lies on the floor, his face badly bruised and swollen, his arm in a sling. He was caught with the other toothpick. Barely able to speak, he guides the Arab with his eyes, leading him to where still another metal pick is hidden.

A policeman comes to take the Arab out. The hoodlum quickly clenches his fist to hide the pick. Billy pleads with the Arab to contact Maurice Portnoy for him on the outside. They have difficulty communicating, but Billy repeats Portnoy's number over and over.

Cut to Siddy dialing the same number, getting Portnoy's secretary. He is out. She leaves a message that Billy is missing.

Cut to the Arab leaving the cell. Square and Billy are convinced he hasn't understood them. There is a scene between the boys and the hoodlum. Billy talks of running away again. Square says, "Where will you go this time, Siberia?" The hoodlum laughs and says, "The Cameroons, where everyone is black." Billy tells him to shut up, and Square tries to calm him down. The hoodlum says: "American boy, listen to me. My mother was poor and my father was somewhere else, and I ran away and I am here, am I not black? I went back when I was your age but my mother was gone and there was no back to go to, and so I am here. When a policeman sees me, I do nothing, I am in jail, am I not black? Go home, boy, go home!"

Billy exclaims: "This isn't America." And the hoodlum responds, "In America they have Negroes and thieves, and here we have Arabs and thieves, there is always someone and thieves, go home." When the hoodlum and Square are through with Billy, he is saying, "Paris is a beautiful city. . . ." The hoodlum says, "Is that a reason to cry?" And Billy finishes, "Paris is a beautiful city but it is not my home."

Billy is surprised to hear he has a visitor. He is taken out of the cell. It is the lawyer, Maurice Portnoy, who didn't believe the Arab, but after getting the message from Siddy that Billy was missing, he decided to come anyway. Maurice and Billy hug each other. Maurice promises to put in a couple of calls, try to get Billy before a judge in two days. Billy says, "Maurice, it's been six days already, has my hair turned white?"

Before leaving, Maurice slips Billy a pack of cigarettes, but as soon as he is gone, the jailer takes the cigarettes away.

Two days later. Billy and Square are hurriedly putting their belts on and lacing their shoes. They are free, after eight days of being treated "just like any Frenchman." They have been acquitted.

Billy is given back his keys, his money, his fountain pen, his wallet. Then his passport is flung on the table before him. The camera comes in close to the passport and we can read the only words on its cover, "The United States of America."

Dissolve to Billy rushing like a madman through the traffic of Paris, his heart a cacophony of all the jazz themes of the film. He reaches Siddy's hotel, knowing she left with her troupe for Rome.

He asks the desk clerk, "Is there a message from Miss St. Clare?"

"No message."

"Did she leave a manuscript?"

"No manuscript."

"No?"

"Nothing."

"Is the troupe gone?"

"Yes, it is gone seven days."

Billy goes to a phone, starts to dial Maurice's number, when he sees a reflection in the glass: Siddy walking into the hotel, carrying the manuscript under her arm, just as he used to. For a moment only, they hesitate before each other like strangers, then suddenly embrace.

"Was it bad?" she asks. "Maurice just told me where you've been."

"Worse," he says, "because I was sure you had gone. Why did you stay?"

She blushes, and to avoid the obvious answer, holds up his manuscript in front of him. "Finish it soon," she says. "It's a marvelous story."

He takes a clean sheet of paper and prints on it carefully, "For Siddy, who waited." "That," he says, "is the dedication page."

Dissolve to the jazz club, New Year's Eve. A very sad blues is being played, and we hear the bass again, as at the beginning. Maurice and Square and Siddy and Billy are seated at one table, as the proprietor comes over and shakes hands warmly with Square. "Ah, my American friend, I knew you wouldn't be away for long."

The proprietor then turns to Siddy.

"Ah, my other American, you are back, too. Good."

He turns to Billy.

"You are an American?"

"Yes," says Billy.

"You are staying here?"

"We've been here," says Billy. He looks at Siddy.

And Siddy says, "We're going home."

We see a close-up of their hands, held tightly together. Then, as the camera dollies quickly back and up, the festivities below become an anonymous swirl of gaiety and noise, over which we hear only the cool, clear tones of Square's clarinet.

The End

EQUAL IN PARIS

by Sol Stein and James Baldwin

Based on the nonfiction story of the same name in
Notes of a Native Son by James Baldwin

CHARACTERS

(In Order of Appearance)

BILLY ADE, A COLORED BOY OF 25

SIDDY ST. CLARE, A COLORED GIRL IN HER LATE
        TEENS

SQUARE, A YOUNG BOHEMIAN WITH A BEARD

A WAITER

FIRST POLICEMAN

SECOND POLICEMAN

THREE PRISONERS: AN ARAB PEANUT VENDOR

                A HOODLUM

                A BOY OF 16

A JAILER

THE PRISON PHOTOGRAPHER

A TYPIST

A HOTEL OWNER

A JUDGE

A PRIEST

MAURICE PORTNOY, A LAWYER

ACT ONE

ON THE DARKENED FLOOR THE CAMERA FINDS A STRIPED
PATTERN; THE SHADOW OF BARS ON A PRISON CELL. THE
CAMERA LIFTS ITS HEAD AS IT WERE, TO DISCOVER, ALSO
IN THE DARKNESS, A MARVELOUS FACE, A NEGRO BOY OF
TWENTY-FIVE WITH LARGE LARGE EYES. HE WEARS A
SWEATER MUCH TOO BIG; PERHAPS IT IS SOMEONE ELSE'S.
A WHITE DICKEY COLLAR SETS OFF HIS FACE, A SAD
BLACK MOON. THE CAMERA MOVES AROUND HIS HEAD IN A
COMPLETE CIRCLE AS IF WE WERE LOOKING AT A PIECE OF
SCULPTURE, WHICH, IN A WAY, WE ARE.

AS THE CAMERA CIRCLES, WE HEAR THE ODDLY PUNCTUATED
LILT OF HIS VOICE.

BILLY'S VOICE: On the nineteenth of December, in
1949, when I had been living in Paris for a little
over a year, I was arrested as a receiver of stolen
goods and spent eight days in prison.

BILLY LIGHTS THE BUTT OF A CIGARETTE WHICH HAS BEEN
SMOKED BEFORE.

The story began, like all terrible things begin,
quietly.

THE BACKGROUND LIGHTS. BILLY IS SEATED AT A SIDE-
WALK CAFE. ON THE TABLE IN FRONT OF HIM, HIS DRINK
AND A PILE OF BOOKS, NINE OR TEN OF THEM. HE IS
SMOKING THE STUB AND FILING HIS NAILS IN A DEFINITE
RHYTHM, THEN STOPS. HE LIFTS THE TOP BOOK AWAY, AND
THEN THE NEXT; REVEALING THE TOP OF A GIRL'S FACE,
A COLORED GIRL OF NOT MORE THAN 19, SEATED AT THE
NEXT TABLE. BILLY REMOVES ANOTHER BOOK AND WE SEE
ALL OF THE GIRL'S FACE. SHE LOOKS AWAY.

BILLY: Hi.

NO RESPONSE.

I said Hi.

SHE NODS SHYLY. BILLY LIFTS AWAY ANOTHER BOOK OR
TWO AND WE SEE THAT THE GIRL'S BELONGINGS INCLUDE
A PORTABLE EASEL: CANVAS, A TIN CAN FULL OF
BRUSHES . . . AND A SWEET SMILE SHE CANNOT HIDE,
HARD AS SHE TRIES.

BILLY: Hi. You must be an American.

SIDDY: Oh yes.

THEN HESITATINGLY.

Are you?

BILLY LAUGHS.

BILLY: I'm a Senegalese.

SIDDY: Oh I'll bet!

BILLY: My father's a headhunter.

SIDDY: Oh I'll bet!

BILLY: You don't believe me?

SIDDY: Senegalese have a lovely lilt in their voice. They speak beautifully. You sound like you're from New Jersey.

BILLY: You win.

WITH A WAVE OF HIS HAND HE TAKES IN HER EASEL AND ACCESSORIES.

You paint?

SIDDY: Well! How'd you guess?

THEY LAUGH. HE POINTS TO THE CANVAS.

BILLY: Can I see it?

SIDDY: It's not much yet.

BILLY:

(IMITATING HER)

Oh I'll bet!

SHE LAUGHS.

Please?

SLOWLY, WORRIED ABOUT HIS REACTION; SIDDY TURNS
THE CANVAS TOWARDS HIM.

Hey, not bad.

SIDDY: Mean it?

BILLY: Do I look like the kind that lies?

SHE LOOKS AT HIM SERIOUSLY.

You're looking at the wrong side of my face. That's
my lying side. Look at this side, it never lies.

SHE LAUGHS AND THE EASEL STARTS TO SLIP. BILLY
QUICKLY HELPS HER WITH IT, THEN SEIZES THE OPPOR-
TUNITY TO MOVE HIS DRINK AND HIMSELF TO HER TABLE.

SIDDY: Is that nice? You've practically picked me
up.

BILLY: Not really. My books are still over there.
Technically, I'm still sitting there. Here I'm
just visiting.

SIDDY: Are you reading all those at the same time?

BILLY: Yes indeed. Terribly disorganized. No powers of concentration. A real failure.

SIDDY: As a reader?

BILLY: As a writer, too. As everything.

HE IS LOST IN SPACE, STARING AT HER.

SIDDY: No powers of concentration.

BILLY: I'm sorry. You've got a lovely face.

SIDDY: Camouflage. For a wicked mind.

BILLY: Oh I'll bet.

THEY LAUGH AGAIN.

SIDDY: You're a writer.

BILLY: How'd you know?

SIDDY: You look like you don't _do_ anything, so I figured you're rich or a writer. You don't look rich.

BILLY: I _am,_ I _am,_ a member of the propertied classes. I own . . .

SIDDY: Yes?

BILLY: A pen. See, it doesn't show but I've got it. And paper, scads of paper.

SIDDY: Anything written on it?

BILLY: Heaps, tons, a novel mostly, and mostly finished too. I give it a week, maybe less.

SIDDY: How long have you been writing it?

BILLY: On paper, seven years, but really <u>always</u>.
Mostly thinking, like painting is mostly looking.

SIDDY: How long have you been here?

BILLY:

(SLYLY)

Are you trying to pick me up?

(LAUGHING)

Over a year.

SIDDY: That's marvelous. I've been in Paris less
than two months and I have to leave already. I wish
it were a year. I love it. I'm going to Switzerland
tomorrow. For a couple of weeks. Then . . . home
on the <u>Liberté</u>.

BILLY: Tomorrow?

SIDDY: Tomorrow and tomorrow and tomorrow, it
comes much too fast. What do you write . . . besides the novel?

BILLY: Poems, songs, unsaleable things. In high school I got a letter of congratulations from Mayor LaGuardia for winning a poetry prize and it went to my head. I haven't stopped writing since. How long have you been painting?

SIDDY: Always. Finger paint, crayons, water colors, now this. Hasn't changed much, has it? My father says, "Crazy girl, what do you want to do <u>that</u> for, you got something against the way things look when you <u>see</u> them?" I like what I see.

BILLY: I like what I see, too. You have nice eyes.

SIDDY: Did your father let you be a writer?

BILLY: Heavens, no, my father wanted me to become a preacher, a bellering, yellering, praise-the-Lord preacher. When I was fourteen I became a preacher. When I was seventeen I stopped. The world's been going to blazes ever since. The world is nothing less than a conspiracy against the cultivation of my talent. Especially since I don't make any money at it. Which is a pity. I love to eat and drink. I love to argue—with people who don't disagree with me too much. And I love to laugh—only the world's in a conspiracy against that too. And I can't make any money at it.

THEY BOTH LAUGH.

This novel might get published, though. It'll be finished in a week.

SIDDY: I hope it's a good week.

BILLY:

(LOOKING AT HER)

It's bound to be. Now.

HE TRIES TO PUT HIS HAND ON HERS, BUT SHE AVOIDS IT GRACEFULLY.

SIDDY: What do you want to be?

BILLY: You mean when I grow up?

SIDDY: Aren't you grown up?

BILLY: I want to be an honest man . . . and a good writer, how's that sound? Look, can I bring my books over?

SIDDY: It's a free country.

BILLY GOES TO GET HIS BOOKS AND PRACTICALLY STUMBLES UPON SQUARE, A WHITE BOY WITH A BOHEMIAN ATTEMPT AT A BEARD.

BILLY: Excuse me.

SQUARE: My fault, old boy, my fault.

HE SEES WHOM HE HAS BUMPED INTO.

My God, Billy Ade, I thought you were in New York.

BILLY: Square.

THEY CLAP EACH OTHER ON THE BACK.

I thought _you_ were in New York.

SQUARE: Well, you're here and I'm here, I guess New York is here. How've you been?

BILLY: Let me introduce—

SQUARE: Imagine, imagine, imagine, meeting you here. Small world.

BILLY: I want to introduce—

SQUARE: Sure, sure . . .

HE GREETS SIDDY.

BILLY: This is . . .

SIDDY: Siddy St. Clare.

SQUARE: Ma'am.

SIDDY: Miss. How do you do?

SQUARE: I do just dandy, stumbling across Billy Ade—imagine! Oh, it's good to see you. Long time, long time, mind if I join? Thanks. What a time. Got here a couple of weeks ago and don't know a soul in town . . .

BILLY: You've grown a beard pretty fast.

SQUARE: Oh this, that's a New York beard. Brought it with me. I'm holed up at a real stinker of a hotel near the Gare St. Lazare, murder. The owner's a thief and his wife's a nymphomaniac, neither of them will leave me alone. And you should see the chambermaids, two to a room, three to a room. Hell, there aren't any chambermaids, where you living?

BILLY: At the Grand Hotel du Bac. It's a joint.

SQUARE: You two together?

SIDDY BLUSHES. BILLY IS ANNOYED.

BILLY: I live at the Bac. We just met.

SQUARE: Good, good, good. They got a room for me?

SIDDY: You people old friends?

BILLY: No, but we're putting on a good show. Always happens abroad, two Americans, wouldn't bother to visit if they lived down the block in New York, meet in Paris and fall into each other's arms. Right?

SQUARE: Wrong. Listen, I've got to get out of that Bigelow Hotel. What a joint.

BILLY: Mine's a joint, too.

SQUARE: Never mind. They must have a room for me.

BILLY: Like she says, it's a free country.

SQUARE: Well let's go, what are we waiting for?
Nice meeting you, Miss.

BILLY:

(TO SIDDY, AS IF APOLOGIZING)

He plays the xylophone.

SIDDY:

(WITH A TOUCH OF IRONY)

An artist!

SQUARE: I play the harp, you know I play the harp.

BILLY: The boy harpist, how could I forget.

(TO SIDDY)

Do you have to see Switzerland?

SIDDY: I have to paint Switzerland.

BILLY: When, what time tomorrow.

SIDDY: Tomorrow?

BILLY: Do you leave?

SIDDY: Tomorrow evening.

BILLY: Listen, can I meet you here tonight, at eight?
Please?

SIDDY: I suppose no harm.

BILLY: No harm, honest. Make it seven?

SQUARE: Come on!

BILLY: Make it seven?

SIDDY: All right.

BILLY BLOWS HER A KISS, KEEPS LOOKING BACK AT HER
AS SQUARE CARTS HIM OFF. DISSOLVE TO HALLWAY OF
HOTEL DU BAC, JUST OUTSIDE BILLY'S ROOM.

BILLY: That's yours down the hall. Fourteen.

SQUARE: E-ternally grateful.

SQUARE LUGS HIS SUITCASES DOWN THE HALL. BILLY EN-
TERS HIS OWN ROOM. THE BED IS UNMADE, THE LINEN
RUMPLED. HE DROPS DOWN ON THE BED, CLOSES HIS EYES,
RESTING FROM SQUARE'S ENTHUSIASM. A KNOCK ON THE
DOOR, AND BEFORE BILLY CAN ANSWER IT SWINGS OPEN.

SQUARE: Me. E-ternally grateful. Wonderful room. Fabulous.

BILLY: Well keep it quiet or they'll raise the rates.

SQUARE SEES THE CRUMPLED BED.

SQUARE: When do they change linen?

BILLY: They _never_ change it. At least if they _made_ the beds, I wouldn't have to look at it.

SQUARE: Solved. Don't breathe. I'll be right back.

SQUARE DARTS OUT. BILLY STARTS PUTTING HIS BOOKS AWAY, BUT SQUARE IS BACK IN THE ROOM ALMOST IMME-DIATELY, A CLEAN, FOLDED SHEET UNDER HIS ARM.

SQUARE: E-ternally grateful. My compliments, to a fellow New Yorker.

BILLY: Oh no!

SQUARE: Oh yes!

HE WHIPS OFF THE SHEET ON BILLY'S BED, BEGINS RE-MAKING IT.

SQUARE: Come on, lend a hand.

BILLY: Sure, sure, but I don't—

SQUARE: Do, don't don't, do. Live it up, I say.

THE BED IS MADE. SQUARE EXAMINES HIS HANDIWORK WITH
GREAT PRIDE.

SQUARE: How about chow?

BILLY: I'm meeting the girl tonight.

SQUARE: Well how about a drink? I'll buy the first
round. I'll buy the second round if it's a cheap
place.

BILLY: Square, I got to do some writing now . . .

SQUARE: Letters can wait.

BILLY: This is a novel and it can't wait. I can't
wait. Besides, I always work on schedule, four
hours in the morning, two in the afternoon, Sundays
included. Always work before I deserve a drink or
dinner.

SQUARE: Always?

BILLY: Always.

SQUARE: I can take a hint, Billy Boy. Knock when
you're through.

HE RAT-A-TATS ON THE DOOR.

I'll treat to two rounds, remember. E-ternally grateful. Boy am I glad we bumped into each other, aren't you?

BILLY STARTS TO SAY SOMETHING BUT SQUARE HAS AL-READY SLAMMED THE DOOR. THEN SQUARE POKES HIS HEAD BACK IN.

I'll treat if it's a <u>cheap</u> place, right?

BILLY: Right.

SQUARE IS OUT AGAIN. BILLY LOOKS AT THE DOOR AS IF HE EXPECTS SQUARE TO BOUNCE BACK IN. SATISFIED THAT HE IS GONE, BILLY GOES TO HIS WORK TABLE AND AMIDST THE MOUNTAINS OF PAPER, STARTS TO WRITE. DISSOLVE ON BILLY ONCE OR TWICE TO INDICATE THE PASSAGE OF TIME. BILLY RUBS HIS EYES, WASHES HIS FACE WITH COLD WATER FROM A BOWL, DRIES HIS FACE, ADJUSTS HIS CLOTHES. AS BACKGROUND, WE HEAR THE SOFT, FAMIL-IAR, DARK-LIGHT STRAIN OF A FRENCH CHANTEUSE. A GLANCE AT HIS WATCH SHOWS BILLY IT'S NEARLY SEVEN. HE GOES DOWN THE HALL TO SQUARE'S ROOM, IS ABOUT TO KNOCK, HESITATES, LOOKS AT HIS WATCH AGAIN, DE-CIDES AGAINST KNOCKING, HEADS FOR THE STAIRS. THE BACKGROUND SONG DISSOLVES THE SCREEN IN SOUND. THE MUSIC STOPS, BECOMES ABSOLUTE SILENCE AS WE SEE SIDDY AT THE CAFE TABLE.

BILLY'S VOICE: Hello. I hardly recognized you without the easel.

WE DO NOT SEE HIM YET.

SIDDY: Well hello Mr. Five-Minutes-Late.

BILLY'S VOICE: I ducked Square.

SIDDY: Who?

WE SEE BILLY NOW AS HE SITS DOWN BESIDE HER.

BILLY: The boy with the beard.

SIDDY: Do you like him?

BILLY: I hardly know him. I couldn't say no about the hotel. Some people are so-o-o sensitive.

SHE LAUGHS.

SIDDY: You hardly know him, what could he expect?

BILLY: I hardly know you.

SIDDY:

(SLYLY)

What do you expect?

BILLY: I expect you're nervous.

SIDDY: You were five minutes late.

BILLY: I'll make up for it. A real special occasion. I brought a tie.

HE TAKES A TIE FROM HIS JACKET POCKET, FROWNS AT IT, PUTS IT BACK IN THE POCKET.

SIDDY:

(LAUGHING)

No respect.

BILLY: Admiration. I'll go get a tux.

SIDDY: There isn't time.

BILLY: You _have_ to leave tomorrow?

HE PUTS HIS HAND ON HERS. CLOSE-UP. SHE STARTS TO PULL AWAY. HIS GRIP IS FIRM.

SIDDY: Is that nice?

BILLY: Very.

SIDDY: Force?

BILLY: I'm a very forceful guy. I've just pulled Switzerland off the map so you can't go.

SIDDY: Well, I'll just get on the train and see.

BILLY: I'll tear up all the tracks.

SIDDY: I'll fly.

BILLY: I'm flying now. Right now. Why'd you come to Paris? Really.

SIDDY: Same reason you did. To get away.

BILLY: You're going back.

SIDDY: I don't think there's anything important you can run away from as long as you carry yourself with you.

BILLY:

(WITH FIERCE DETERMINATION)

I'm not going back.

A WAITER PUTS DRINKS DOWN IN FRONT OF THEM.

SIDDY: Was it rough for you back home?

HE NODS.

And it isn't here?

BILLY: Not easy, but you get treated the same as everybody else.

SIDDY: Does everybody get treated nice here? I hadn't noticed.

BILLY: Can't you stay a while longer, a few weeks maybe. Don't you want to see what Paris is really like?

SIDDY: Ever been in a French hospital? I had three days of it. I know what Paris is really like . . . for the French.

BILLY: I can't agree with a word you say. I never met a girl like you before, I think. . . .

SIDDY: I think we'd better try the wine.

BILLY: I know the wine. It's you I'd like to know better.

SIDDY: Better try the wine.

RELUCTANTLY, HE TEASES HER, DECIDES TO INTERTWINE THEIR ARMS FOR THE FIRST SIP. AS THEIR ARMS LINK, BILLY GENTLY KISSES HER.

SIDDY: Slow down, you're running.

BILLY: You're leaving.

THEN IT HAPPENS. ENTANGLED, HER GLASS UPSETS, SPILLS OVER HER DRESS.

BILLY: Oh my! I'm sorry.

SIDDY: Just look at me.

SHE IS NEAR TEARS.

I won't have time to get it cleaned before I leave.

BILLY: Try cold water fast.

SIDDY: All over this? I'll be soaking. Listen, I've got to run to the hotel. Don't mind the dress, I'll get it out.

SHE GETS UP.

BILLY: I'll come with you.

SIDDY: You know that isn't possible.

THEY STAND FACING EACH OTHER.

BILLY: Everything is possible.

SIDDY: I'll see you in New York.

BILLY: I'm not going back.

SIDDY: Everyone learns to go home.

BILLY: Not there. Not me.

SIDDY: I'll give you my address in New York.

BILLY:

(DESPERATELY)

Meet me here. Later.

SIDDY: I can't. I've promised dinner to a friend.

BILLY:

(HURT)

A man friend?

SIDDY:

(LAUGHING)

A woman friend. I like you.

BILLY: Meet me here tomorrow, before the train.

SIDDY: And spot another dress.

BILLY: Please? At three?

SIDDY: You won't get your novel finished at that rate.

BILLY: Blast the novel!

SIDDY: You don't mean that.

BILLY: I mean this.

GENTLY, HE TAKES HER IN HIS ARMS, AND GENTLY KISSES HER.

SIDDY:

(CLOSE-UP OF HER LIPS NEAR HIS EAR)

Tomorrow at three.

DISSOLVE ON BILLY'S JOYOUS FACE. BACK AT HIS HOTEL, HE IS GOING DOWN THE HALL TO SQUARE'S ROOM. HE KNOCKS ON THE DOOR. A MOMENT OF SILENCE.

SQUARE'S VOICE: Who's that?

BILLY: Ethel Waters. It's me, you dope. Sorry I'm late.

BILLY PUSHES THE DOOR OPEN, REVEALING SQUARE AND TWO FRENCH POLICEMEN. THEY ARE EXAMINING SQUARE'S IDENTIFICATION PAPERS.

FIRST POLICEMAN: Hello.

BILLY: Hello.

THE SECOND POLICEMAN SHUTS THE DOOR BEHIND BILLY.

BILLY: What's up? What gives?

SQUARE: God knows, kid, they're looking for some kind of gangster, I guess. No gangsters here, right Billy Boy? I guess they've seen too many French detective movies, right? Ha, ha, ha.

BILLY: Ha, ha, let's go to dinner. Big joke. This time I'm hungry.

FIRST POLICEMAN: One moment.

BILLY: I could use a drink.

FIRST POLICEMAN: Your identification papers. Please.

BILLY: Sure, sure, what's up.

POLICEMAN TAKES THE PAPERS, EXAMINES THEM.

FIRST POLICEMAN: Can we see your room?

BILLY: Now?

SECOND POLICEMAN: I think now.

BILLY: It's not very presentable.

FIRST POLICEMAN: I think we would like to see your room, yes?

BILLY LOOKS AT SQUARE. SQUARE DROPS HIS SHOULDERS.

BILLY: I guess okay. Why not?

FIRST POLICEMAN: Come.

THEY GO DOWN THE HALL.

You are not from Paris originally?

BILLY: Originally I'm from New York.

SECOND POLICEMAN: New York, they say, is a lovely city.

BILLY: Paris is a lovely city.

SQUARE: Sure, the weather's great. Fabulous.

BILLY: You'd never know it was almost Christmas.

THEY ENTER BILLY'S ROOM. THE FIRST POLICEMAN IN-STANTLY GOES TO THE BED, LIFTS THE PILLOW, AND AT ONCE BILLY REALIZES WHAT HAS HAPPENED. ON THE NEW BEDSHEET THE WORDS "HOTEL BIGELOW" STAND OUT LARGE AND CLEAR.

BILLY: Now wait a minute, before anyone blows his top, I can explain. It isn't . . .

FIRST POLICEMAN: Yes?

BILLY LOOKS AT SQUARE.

BILLY: Nothing. Look, in America, guests in hotels often take soap and ashtrays and towels. It's a cus-tom. You know the meaning of custom?

FIRST POLICEMAN: A sheet is a custom?

BILLY: Not exactly.

FIRST POLICEMAN: I'm so sorry, but you'll have to come with us. Both of you.

THE POLICEMEN REMOVE THE SHEET, FOLD THE EVIDENCE
NEATLY, PREPARE TO GO.

BILLY: But is this very serious?

FIRST POLICEMAN: No, it's not serious.

SECOND POLICEMAN: It is nothing at all.

SQUARE: I guess we're going to catch hell. I bet
we're going to get the biggest bawling out all in
French.

BILLY: Will this take very long? I don't like having dinner _that_ late. How long will this take?

FIRST POLICEMAN: Who knows how long what will take?

DISSOLVE TO ROOM IN POLICE STATION. THERE IS A
DESK, BUT NO ONE BEHIND IT.

SECOND POLICEMAN: The man in authority is not here.

SQUARE: Well, we'll come back whenever you say.

FIRST POLICEMAN: Oh no, that is not what is possible.

SQUARE: Hey, this isn't exactly what I'd call in
the spirit of Lafayette. My friend here from New
York is a very impatient man, and I'm an impatient
man, and we'll just have ourselves a dinner some-
place close and come back. . . .

HE IS WALKING TOWARDS THE DOOR WHEN THE FIRST PO-
LICEMAN LAYS A HAND ON HIS SHOULDER, GENTLY. THE
HAND IS REMOVED JUST AS SOON AS IT'S PUT ON.

BILLY: Well. I guess we all wait.

FIRST POLICEMAN: I'm afraid that is not what is
possible. We can't wait. Please be as kind as to
come with us.

BILLY: What about our dinner?

FIRST POLICEMAN: In time. Come.

BILLY:

(FRIGHTENED NOW)

Where are we going?

ONE POLICEMAN TAKES BILLY, THE OTHER SQUARE, BY THE
ARM.

BILLY: Hey, I said where are we going?

CUT TO JAIL CORRIDOR.

BILLY: Mister, I want to call my embassy.

FIRST POLICEMAN: Yes, yes. Later.

SQUARE: What do you mean, later. Now.

SECOND POLICEMAN: Shh, some of the prisoners are asleep.

SQUARE: I don't give a- Look, I don't care if I wake the whole place up and down, see!

FIRST POLICEMAN: Some of these men are not gentlemen. They would not be kind to you if you wake them up.

THEY'RE STOPPED IN FRONT OF A CELL.

BILLY: I want to call a lawyer.

FIRST POLICEMAN: Yes, yes. Later.

BILLY: You can't keep us incommunicado.

SECOND POLICEMAN: Perhaps the gentleman is not aware of the laws of France?

THE POLICEMAN HAS OPENED THE DOOR OF THE CELL. THE CAMERA MOVES IN QUICKLY. THERE ARE THREE OCCU-PANTS—A SEEDY ARAB PEANUT VENDOR, A YOUNG BOY OF SIXTEEN OR SO, AND A HOODLUM WHO SITS PICKING AT HIS DECAYED TEETH WITH A METAL TOOTHPICK. AS SOON AS HE SEES THE POLICEMAN, HE PUTS THE PICK AWAY. THE CAMERA TAKES IN THE STONE WALL BEHIND THEM, AROUND THEM, THE DIRTY FLOOR, STOPS AND STARES AT THE SINGLE BARE BULB IN THE CEILING. SUDDENLY THE 16-YEAR-OLD BOY RUSHES AT THE POLICEMAN, STARTS PUNCHING HIM WITH HIS FISTS. WITH A SINGLE WHACK, THE POLICEMAN SENDS THE BOY SPRAWLING.

BOY: My father will kill you.

SECOND POLICEMAN:

(LAUGHING)

You don't have a father.

BOY: I'll kill you.

SECOND POLICEMAN: Yes, yes, you'll kill everybody one day. Meanwhile you're here.

WE ARE NOW IN THE CELL WITH BILLY AND SQUARE LOOKING OUT AT THE POLICEMEN.

BILLY: When are you coming back for us?

FIRST POLICEMAN: Who knows!

THE ARAB PEANUT VENDOR LAUGHS, IS STOPPED IN MID-LAUGH BY THE STARE OF THE POLICEMAN.

BILLY: Look, please, everybody, try to understand. I've got the most important meeting of my life tomorrow.

FIRST POLICEMAN: A meeting can wait.

BILLY:

(NEAR TEARS)

She won't know. I won't know where to find her.
Please, let me at least call somebody, please,
please, please.

SECOND POLICEMAN:

(SOMEWHAT ANGRILY)

What's so special about you? You wait like everybody else. You get treated like everybody else.

A TOUCH OF TERROR COMES TO BILLY'S EYES.

BILLY: But you can't do this. I'm an American.

POLICEMAN: <u>Bon.</u> You are an American.

HE SLAMS THE DOOR SHUT. FADE OUT.

ACT TWO

FADE IN ON THE NAKED LIGHT BULB (LIT) IN THE CEIL-
ING OF THE CELL. IT GOES OUT, SNAPPED OFF BY A MAS-
TER SWITCH SOMEWHERE OUTSIDE. ALL FIVE OCCUPANTS
ARE ASLEEP ON STRAW PALLETS ON THE FLOOR. THE ARAB,
THE BOY, AND THE HOODLUM STIR. WE HEAR THE DISTANT
SOUNDS OF PRISONERS AWAKING ELSEWHERE. BILLY AND
SQUARE, USED TO THE GETTING-UP HOURS OF BOHEMIA,
NOT PRISON, CONTINUE TO SLEEP. THE HOODLUM
SEARCHES IN HIS SHIRT POCKET FOR THE METAL TOOTH-
PICK, PUTS IT IN HIS MOUTH; WALKS OVER TO WHERE
BILLY IS SLEEPING AND NUDGES HIM WITH HIS FOOT.

BILLY: Hey?

HE OPENS HIS EYES. HE DOESN'T QUITE REMEMBER YET
WHERE HE IS. THE HOODLUM POINTS TO THE CEILING
LIGHT, NO LONGER LIT, TO THE BARRED WINDOW WHERE
SOME EARLY MORNING LIGHT CAN BE SEEN DESPITE A DE-
PRESSING RAINFALL. THE ARAB SCRATCHES HIMSELF
AWAKE. BILLY SHAKES SQUARE.

BILLY: Come on, man.

SQUARE:

(YAWNS)

BILLY: No, we're somewhere's else. Come on, we've got to find a way to get out of here. Get your corpse out of bed.

SQUARE: Bed, you call this a bed?

BILLY: What do you expect, sheets?

SQUARE: What's eating you?

BILLY: I had a wonderful night. I love it here. I can't think of anyplace else I'd rather be. I could break your neck. What made you steal a sheet for, idiot?

SQUARE: I didn't steal it, I took it.

BILLY: You gave the landlord a receipt.

SQUARE: Listen, that landlord's a thief.

BILLY: He's a thief. He took your sheet?

SQUARE: I told you his wife wouldn't let me alone.

BILLY: So you took the sheet. That makes real sense.

SQUARE: Look, Billy Boy, that's spilt milk, see, now let's concentrate on getting out . . .

BILLY: Like a bird, sure, sure, <u>how?</u> You're the bearded prophet, you tell me!

SQUARE: Take it easy, kid. We'll get a lawyer.

BILLY: You heard the cop. This is France. They'll let you see a lawyer when they're good and ready. And they're not ready.

SQUARE: We'll call the embassy.

BILLY: What are you going to use for a telephone, your beard?

SQUARE: Lay off!

BILLY: Why didn't you stay home in New York. Nobody bothered you there, did they? Listen, I've got a date with that sugar sweet girl, see, and if I miss that date I'll personally shrink your head to the size of a baseball and give it to the first souvenir hunter I meet, so help me. Shrinking heads is a hereditary talent and I can do it just fine, real fine. Square, you been in jail before?

SQUARE:

(SHAKES HIS HEAD)

Uh uh. Were you?

BILLY: The way some people back home look at me it's like I was.

SQUARE: What do you mean by that?

BILLY: Nothing, forget it.

BILLY TURNS AWAY. SQUARE, NOW AT THE JUDAS HOLE, YELLS.

SQUARE: Hey!

THE ARAB LAUGHS. IN THE CORRIDOR WE SEE THE JAILER TRUNDLING ALONG THREE GARBAGE CANS ON WHEELS. FROM THE FIRST CAN A SORT OF BREAD, IN FIVE PIECES, IS PASSED THROUGH THE JUDAS. FROM THE SECOND CAN, COF-FEE, A TINCAN FULL FOR EACH PRISONER. FROM THE THIRD A THICK LIQUID.

SQUARE: What's this?

THE ARAB: La soupe.

SQUARE: Soup?! Look at this stuff, it must have started cooking before the revolution.

BILLY: You're supposed to eat it. It's part of the punishment. I didn't do anything to get punished for. You eat mine.

SQUARE: You'll be hungry.

BILLY: I am hungry.

THEY MAKE A STAB AT EATING THE MESS, DIPPING THE BREAD IN THE COFFEE, AND IMITATING THE OTHER PRIS-

ONERS, WHO HAVE BECOME ADEPT AT PICKING THE SOLID
MATTER OUT OF THE "SOUP." SUDDENLY A RATTLING, THE
DOOR OPENS, AND THE TWO POLICEMEN APPEAR.

FIRST POLICEMAN: Good morning, I hope you have had
a nice night, please come with us.

SQUARE AND BILLY LOOK AT EACH OTHER WITH GREAT RE-
LIEF. BEFORE THEY ARE OUT OF THE CELL, THE OTHER
PRISONERS ARE DIVIDING UP BILLY'S AND SQUARE'S
FOOD. CUT TO A ROOM ELSEWHERE IN THE PRISON. SQUARE
IS HAVING HIS PICTURE TAKEN AND BILLY IS BEING FIN-
GERPRINTED.

FIRST POLICEMAN:

(TO BILLY, WHILE FILLING OUT THE FORM)

Your age?

BILLY: When do we get out of here?

FIRST POLICEMAN: Your age?

BILLY: I gotta get out of here before three o'clock.
Understand? One, two, three!

FIRST POLICEMAN: Silence. Answer the question.

BILLY: What was the question?

FIRST POLICEMAN: Your age?

BILLY: Twenty-five.

FIRST POLICEMAN: Your height?

BILLY: Five nine.

FIRST POLICEMAN: Good, your weight?

BILLY: 135. If I ate the food you serve here for a while, it'd be a lot less.

FIRST POLICEMAN: Color of your hair.

BILLY: Purple.

THE FIRST POLICEMAN LOOKS UP.

All right, black. Black, black, black. What does it look like?

FIRST POLICEMAN: Why are you so bitter?

BILLY: Why? Why? Look at the way we're treated!

FIRST POLICEMAN: Everybody is treated the same.

BILLY: Like this?

FIRST POLICEMAN: If they steal.

BILLY: I didn't steal!

PHOTOGRAPHER: Next.

HE SHUFFLES BILLY INTO PLACE AND THEY LOOK AT OTHER
OVER THE TOP OF THE ANTIQUATED CAMERA WITH MUTUAL
HATRED. A LIGHT FLASHES.

PHOTOGRAPHER: Sideways!

BILLY TURNS FOR A PROFILE VIEW. A LIGHT FLASHES.

PHOTOGRAPHER: Finished.

THE POLICEMAN HANDCUFFS BILLY AND SQUARE. DISSOLVE
TO THE ROOM WHERE THEY FIRST ENTERED THE PRISON THE
PREVIOUS EVENING. BEHIND THE DESK THERE IS NOW A
MAN-IN-AUTHORITY. NEAR HIM, A GIRL AT A TYPEWRITER
RECORDS EVERYTHING THAT IS SAID.

MAN IN AUTHORITY:

(TO THE POLICEMAN)

These are the criminals?

FIRST POLICEMAN: Yes, sir.

BILLY: What's that you said?!

MAN IN AUTHORITY: Quiet! Where is the accuser?

THE SECOND POLICEMAN BRINGS FORWARD THE OWNER OF
THE BIGELOW HOTEL.

MAN IN AUTHORITY: Where is the evidence?

THE HOTEL OWNER SHOWS THE FOLDED SHEET.

MAN IN AUTHORITY:

(TO SQUARE)

Who stole it, you?

THE HOTEL OWNER NODS HIS HEAD.

SQUARE: I didn't steal anything, I borrowed it.

MAN IN AUTHORITY: Did you have permission for bor-
rowing?

HOTEL OWNER: No, no!!

MAN IN AUTHORITY: Then you stole it.

BILLY: Now wait a minute.

MAN IN AUTHORITY: Did you steal it?

BILLY: No.

MAN IN AUTHORITY: Good, then the other stole it.
This one . . .

(POINTS TO BILLY)

is the receleur.

HOTEL OWNER: Receiver of stolen goods.

MAN IN AUTHORITY: Who made the arrest.

FIRST POLICEMAN: We did, sir.

MAN IN AUTHORITY: Good. Finished.

(TO TYPIST)

You have everything?

TYPIST: Yes, sir.

SHE ZIPS THE PAPER OUT OF THE MACHINE AND HANDS IT TO HIM.

MAN IN AUTHORITY: Both of you sign.

BILLY: Go to blazes!

SQUARE: Cut it out, Billy.

BILLY: I want to see a lawyer.

MAN IN AUTHORITY: Later. Sign.

BILLY: I'm an American. I want to telephone my embassy. Now.

MAN IN AUTHORITY: Later. Sign.

SQUARE: What kind of trial is this? I never heard of such a thing.

MAN IN AUTHORITY: This is a procès-verbal. The trial will be later. Sign.

BILLY: I'm not signing anything.

MAN IN AUTHORITY: I am a very patient man. I will wait ten seconds till you sign.

BILLY: You can't do this!

MAN IN AUTHORITY: Young man, I do what I do. I do it ten hours a day and then I go home to my family. I have six children, all girls. I am a very patient man. Sign.

BILLY: Is this fair?

MAN IN AUTHORITY: I have six girls. Is that fair?

BILLY: What about my rights? I'm an American.

MAN IN AUTHORITY: You are getting the same treatment every Frenchman gets.

BILLY: Now that's real equal. Listen, I've got to get out of here before three o'clock.

MAN IN AUTHORITY: Is it very important?

BILLY: What do you think?

MAN IN AUTHORITY: You have an appointment with the men to whom you sell the bedsheet?

(TO TYPIST)

He has more to tell.

SHE INSERTS PAPER IN THE MACHINE.

SQUARE: This is crazy.

MAN IN AUTHORITY: Please be good boys and sign. Others are waiting.

BILLY: If I sign will it get us out faster?

MAN IN AUTHORITY: Everything is always faster when one cooperates. Sign.

BILLY: Give me that.

OUTRAGED AND FURIOUS, HE SIGNS AND PASSES THE PAPER TO SQUARE. AS SOON AS SQUARE SIGNS, THE MAN THROWS THE PAPER IN A DESK DRAWER.

MAN IN AUTHORITY: Next.

BILLY: Like that?

MAN IN AUTHORITY: Comme ça. Next.

BILLY: When do we get out?

MAN IN AUTHORITY: You know that is not my affair. Next!

194

SQUARE AND BILLY, STILL HANDCUFFED, ARE LED OUT BY THE POLICEMEN. AS THEY PASS THE HOTEL OWNER HE WINKS SLYLY, LAUGHS. AS THE BOYS PASS OUT THE DOOR, THE CAMERA HOLDS ON A SEAL ABOVE THE DOOR: "LIB-ERTÉ, EGALITÉ, FRATERNITÉ."

DISSOLVE TO THE ROOM WHERE THEIR PHOTOS WERE TAKEN.

SECOND POLICEMAN: Your shoelaces.

BILLY: Look, we're due to get a trial, right, and then out, right.

SECOND POLICEMAN: One day you will come to trial.

BILLY: One day!

SECOND POLICEMAN: The time is not my affair. Your shoelaces.

SQUARE: What do you want our shoelaces for?

THE POLICEMAN GESTURES TO INDICATE THEY MIGHT HANG THEMSELVES.

BILLY: What makes you think I'd want to hang myself? I didn't do anything.

THE POLICEMAN SHRUGS HIS SHOULDERS, POINTS TO THE SHOELACES. BILLY AND SQUARE REMOVE THEM. THE PO-LICEMAN DROPS THE LACES INTO A PAPER BAG ON WHICH HE WRITES A CODE NUMBER IN CRAYON.

SECOND POLICEMAN: Belt.

BILLY: How am I going to hold my pants up?

SECOND POLICEMAN: With your hand.

FIRST POLICEMAN: Come, be quick.

THEY REMOVE THEIR BELTS AND BILLY EXPERIENCES THE
HUMILIATION OF TRYING TO KEEP HIS PANTS ON AS HE
SHUFFLES ABOUT IN THE LACELESS SHOES. THE FIRST PO-
LICEMAN LOOKS AT SQUARE'S WRISTS, THEN BILLY'S,
SEES BILLY'S WATCH.

FIRST POLICEMAN: Watch.

BILLY: How will I know what time it is?

SECOND POLICEMAN: When the sun rises it is morning.
When it sets it is evening. Your watch.

BILLY IS SWEATING, SERIOUS. HIS VOICE TREMBLES. HE
SPEAKS QUIETLY AS THE CAMERA STUDIES HIS FACE.

BILLY: I've got a date at three o'clock.

HE LOOKS AT EACH POLICEMAN IN TURN. BOTH SHRUG
THEIR SHOULDERS.

SECOND POLICEMAN: It is the law.

BILLY:

(QUIETLY)

I have a date with a girl. She leaves for Switzerland today.

SECOND POLICEMAN: I'm sorry she leaves for
Switzerland.

BILLY TURNS HIS QUIETNESS INTO A FURY AGAINST
SQUARE.

BILLY: You and your sheet!

SQUARE: You took it!

BILLY: How was I supposed to know it was stolen?
How was I supposed to know you were a crook?

THEY WOULD COME TO BLOWS IF IT WEREN'T FOR THE AWK-
WARDNESS OF TRYING TO KEEP THEIR LACELESS AND BELT-
LESS CLOTHES IN PLACE. THE POLICEMEN HOLD THEM
APART. BILLY BURSTS INTO TEARS.

FIRST POLICEMAN: Oh please do not cry.

BILLY:

(CRYING)

I'm not crying!

THE POLICEMAN OFFERS HIM A CLEAN HANDKERCHIEF.
BILLY SPURNS IT, SNIFFS BACK HIS TEARS.

FIRST POLICEMAN: Finished? Good.

BILLY: What time is it?

FIRST POLICEMAN: Two.

BILLY: In an hour it will be three.

FIRST POLICEMAN: In two hours it will be four, in four hours it will be six, that is the way time is.

Come.

AS BILLY SHUFFLES AWAY, HE STARTS TO STEP OUT OF A SHOE, GRABS FOR IT, AND STARTS TO LOSE HIS PANTS. HE IS TRAPPED IN HIS EMBARRASSMENT. THE POLICEMEN CANNOT KEEP THEMSELVES FROM LAUGHING. THE CAMERA FOCUSES ON AN EXTREME CLOSE-UP OF THEIR LAUGHING FACES, MOUTHS, CUTTING BETWEEN THEM, THEN TO THE CELL . . . THE DOOR CLANGING SHUT BEHIND BILLY AND SQUARE. FOR THE FIRST TIME THEY NOTICE THAT THE OTHER PRISONERS ARE WITHOUT THEIR LACES AND BELTS ALSO. THE FIRST POLICEMAN'S FACE APPEARS AT THE JUDAS. ANGER. HE COMES BACK INTO THE CELL, GOES STRAIGHT TO THE HOODLUM AND TAKES THE METAL TOOTH-PICK FROM HIM. THE HOODLUM MUTTERS AN OATH, BUT AS SOON AS THE POLICEMAN LEAVES, HE SHRUGS HIS SHOUL-DERS, GOES OVER TO A CRACK IN THE WALL AND REMOVES ANOTHER METAL PICK HE HAD HIDDEN THERE, THEN CON-TINUES CALMLY PICKING AT HIS TEETH. THE ARAB IS DE-LOUSING HIS JACKET. THE SIXTEEN YEAR OLD SITS PICKING HIS NOSE, AS IF THAT IS WHERE HIS FUTURE LIES.

HOODLUM:

(TO BILLY)

I was saying, to steal from an American, among my friends, is considered a disgrace. Americans are naive.

BILLY: Do you disgrace yourself often?

THE HOODLUM LAUGHS UPROARIOUSLY.

HOODLUM: You are very clever. On the black market you could do very well.

BILLY: As well as you are doing?

HOODLUM: Ho, ho, ho-much better.

SQUARE: When do we eat? We were supposed to eat hours ago.

HOODLUM: You depend too much on eating. Also an American fault.

BILLY: When do we eat?

HOODLUM: Sometimes earlier, sometimes later. French prisons are not so efficient.

ARAB: Sometimes they forget.

HOODLUM: Oh yes! Do you know, I lost a friend once, a petty thief so petty few of my friends would be seen talking to him, yet in prison one day he was taken out of his cell and he found himself on the wrong line and was guillotined, yes!

THE ARAB AND THE SIXTEEN YEAR OLD JOIN THE HOODLUM IN HIS LAUGHTER. SUDDENLY SQUARE IS LAUGHING WITH THEM. BILLY WHIRLS AROUND TO FACE SQUARE'S GRIN- NING FACE.

BILLY: What do you know? What are you laughing at, goat beard? I've been in the wrong line, I know what it feels like when nothing, you've done noth- ing and you're in the wrong line. Like now. That's what I ran away from and wham! I'm right back where I started, just because you're a punk who steals things for kicks.

SQUARE: Cut it, you're breaking my heart, it's bleeding for you.

CUT RAPIDLY FROM THE HOODLUM TO THE ARAB TO THE BOY, ALL WATCHING TO SEE WHAT WILL HAPPEN, RELISHING THE EXCITEMENT, EGGING THEM ON WITH THEIR GRUNTS.

SQUARE: You missed a date with a broad. One date, one broad, and you yell your head off. What would you be doing if you weren't in jail, smooching with the broad or writing that novel nobody wants to read???

BILLY: I write what I write because I want to write it and I don't give a blessed bit for who reads it or not. It'd be finished if you kept your hands off other people's things.

SQUARE: <u>Your</u> novel, <u>your</u> so-what novel. I never met such a self-centered, whining, self-pitying guy in all my life! Don't you ever think of anybody except yourself?

BILLY: Me? You see what I got all over me, this black? That's right, stare at it! I came here because I didn't want everybody to stare when they saw it. I didn't want people to look at me, I wanted them to forget me, and what do you do? You, you grow a beard so <u>everybody'll</u> notice you. They don't notice your harp-playing, but they'll notice you all right when you parade around looking like a goat!

THIS HITS SQUARE WHERE HE LIVES.

SQUARE:

(BURNING WITH ANGER)

You just watch, you just hold what you're saying, you watch or I'll—

BILLY: I'm watching you. Look at me everybody, I've got a beard!

THIS IS SOMETHING SQUARE CANNOT TAKE. HE RUSHES AT BILLY.

SQUARE: You . . . !

BILLY: I dare you say it!

THEY GRAPPLE, FIGHTING TO THE SOUND OF RAUCOUS EN-
JOYMENT FROM THE OTHER PRISONERS.

BOY: Hit him! Hit him!

ARAB: Good, good!

HOODLUM: When Americans kill each other, the whole
world watches.

WITH A SMASHING BLOW, BILLY SENDS SQUARE SPRAWLING
ACROSS THE CELL. BILLY MOVES IN FAST, STRADDLES
SQUARE, TWISTS HIS ARM. CLOSE-UP OF SQUARE'S FACE.
BILLY'S FACE BREATHING HARD.

SQUARE:

(IN PAIN)

Okay, let go.

BILLY TWISTS HARDER.

SQUARE: Okay, okay. Uncle.

BILLY LETS GO OF SQUARE'S ARM, STANDS UP. SQUARE
FIGHTS TO HOLD BACK TEARS. HE SPEAKS QUIETLY BE-
TWEEN SNIFFLES.

Why . . . did you ever stop to think why I grew a
beard, that maybe it's camouflage, that maybe I
needed it, like you'd like to pick a color that
wasn't black?

BILLY, STILL BREATHING HARD, STARES AT HIM.

SQUARE: I didn't want to leave home, Paris scares
the wits out of me. I can't pat my misery on the
back because I'm not white. What's it to you if I
want to play a harp? You write a novel, okay, okay,
I want to play a harp, so what skin's it off your
back? You don't like anybody calling you black,
sure, but when you saw me, what you said was—the
boy harpist. When you ran away from home, what were
you running from, guys like yourself who cry about
their own warts and laugh at everybody else's, is
that it!?

THE PRISONERS STARE AT BILLY IN HIS SHAME. SUDDENLY
A CLANGING AT THE DOOR AND THE JAILER APPEARS.

JAILER:

(POINTING TO BILLY, SQUARE, AND THE 16 YEAR OLD)

Vous préparez. Vous êtes extraits.

BILLY:

(IN PANIC)

What does he mean?

HOODLUM: Who knows? Maybe the guillotine.

THE PRISONERS LAUGH. THE TWO POLICEMEN ENTER THE
CELL.

HOODLUM: It is a reward for fighting.

HE DOUBLES UP IN LAUGHTER AT HIS OWN JOKE.

FIRST POLICEMAN:

(TO THE HOODLUM)

Shut up!

THE POLICEMEN HANDCUFF BILLY, SQUARE, AND THE BOY, AND THEN TAKE THEM AWAY. DISSOLVE TO A POLICE WAGON OUT-OF-DOORS IN A DRIVING RAIN. THEIR HANDCUFFS ARE TAKEN OFF AND THEY ARE SHOVED THROUGH THE OPEN DOORS OF THE WAGON. INSIDE, A NARROW AISLE AND ON EACH SIDE DOORS LEADING TO A NARROW CUBICLE JUST LARGE ENOUGH FOR A MAN. BILLY, SQUARE, AND THE BOY ARE PUT IN SEPARATE CUBICLES. THE DOORS SLAM SHUT.

BILLY'S VOICE: I'm sorry, Square.

SQUARE'S VOICE: It's okay, kid.

CUT TO A CLOSE-UP OF THE WAGON'S EXHAUST AS THE EN-GINE IS STARTED UP. CUT TO A CLOSE-UP OF BILLY'S FACE. CUT TO THE EXHAUST AGAIN, A BILLOW OF SMOKE WHICH DISSOLVES TO A RAMSHACKLE COURTROOM, A JUDGE ON A HIGH BENCH. THE BOY IS THRUST BEFORE THE BENCH FIRST. THE CAMERA DOLLIES BACK UNTIL IT IS BEHIND BILLY AND SQUARE. WE ONLY HEAR FAINTLY WHAT IS GOING ON UP FRONT. THE PROCEDURE TAKES ONLY SEC-ONDS. A FEW SENTENCES ARE CLEAR ENOUGH TO BE HEARD.

JUDGE: Stealing a sweater.

CLOSE-UP, OF THE BOY, DEFIANT.

JUDGE: I said stealing a sweater.

THE BOY SPITS ON THE FLOOR.

Six months.

THE BOY IS FORCIBLY TAKEN AWAY, HURLING HATRED WITH
HIS EYES AND VOICE, A STRING OF CURSES TIED AROUND
THE ONLY WORLD HE KNOWS.

JUDGE: These two, they are together?

FIRST POLICEMAN: Yes, your honor. This one stole,
this one received.

JUDGE: It says here they are Americans. Where is
the interpreter?

FIRST POLICEMAN: Interpreter?

HE LOOKS AT THE SECOND POLICEMAN.

SECOND POLICEMAN: Interpreter?

JUDGE: Idiots, there must be an interpreter for
Americans. Take them back.

BILLY: No! I don't need an interpreter. I live in
Paris.

JUDGE: This is your home?

BILLY: I am living here.

JUDGE: And stealing here?

BILLY: I didn't steal.

JUDGE: Boys should stay at home. You _are_ an American, yes?

BILLY LOOKS AT SQUARE.

BILLY: Yes.

JUDGE: The law says you must have an interpreter. Tomorrow is Christmas. You will be brought back after Christmas . . . with an interpreter.

BILLY: I don't want to be in jail on Christmas.

JUDGE: The world, my son, you are old enough to know this, is not made up of institutions designed to fulfill one's wants. Take them away.

SQUARE AND BILLY ARE HANDCUFFED TOGETHER AND TAKEN FROM THE ROOM, THE CAMERA FOCUSED ON BILLY'S BLACK HAND HANDCUFFED TO THE WHITE HAND OF SQUARE, BOUND TOGETHER. FADE OUT.

ACT THREE

BILLY AND SQUARE ARE BEING THRUST BACK INTO THEIR
CELL. THE ARAB SITS WRAPPING SOME THINGS IN A KER-
CHIEF. THEY ARE SURPRISED TO SEE THE HOODLUM LYING
ON THE FLOOR, HIS FACE BADLY BRUISED AND SWOLLEN,
HIS ARM IN A SLING.

SQUARE: What happened to him?

THE ARAB SHAKES HIS HEAD SADLY.

SQUARE: Did he fall?

THE ARAB LAUGHS.

THE HOODLUM MUMBLES. SQUARE AND BILLY DROP DOWN
CLOSE TO HIM SO THEY CAN HEAR HIM SPEAK.

HOODLUM: They found . . .

THE ARAB LAUGHS.

HOODLUM: They . . . found . . . the . . .

BILLY: What happened?

THE HOODLUM GESTURES AT HIS TEETH.

The toothpick? They found the toothpick?

THE HOODLUM NODS, DROPS HIS HEAD BACK EXHAUSTED
FROM THE ORDEAL OF TRYING TO SPEAK.

BILLY: Just for that?

THE ARAB SHRUGS HIS SHOULDERS. HE HAS FINISHED
WRAPPING HIS THINGS IN THE KERCHIEF.

ARAB: Au revoir.

THE HOODLUM IS TRYING TO SAY SOMETHING. THEY BEND
CLOSE.

HOODLUM: His time . . . is up.

THE ARAB SMILES.

ARAB: I go.

HE LEANS OVER THE HOODLUM.

I do for you? Pour vous?

THE HOODLUM NODS. HE TRIES TO INDICATE SOMETHING.
FOR A MOMENT THE ARAB IS PUZZLED, THEN HE COMPRE-
HENDS THE REQUEST, SMILES. GUIDED BY THE EYES OF
THE HOODLUM, HE FINDS A CREVICE IN THE WALL WHERE
A THIRD METAL TOOTHPICK HAS BEEN HIDDEN. HE GIVES
IT TO THE HOODLUM, WHO TAKES IT GRATEFULLY WITH HIS

GOOD HAND. WE HEAR THE JAILER COMING. THE HOODLUM
CLENCHES HIS FIST TO HIDE THE PICK. THE ARAB PRE-
PARES TO LEAVE.

BILLY: Please, you must do something for me.

THE ARAB LOOKS AT HIM.

Please, this is very important. You're going outside.

THE ARAB NODS.

SQUARE: Really outside?

BILLY: Let me handle this. I hope to God he can understand me.

(TO THE ARAB)

There is a man, un homme, the only one in Paris who
can help me, a lawyer, avocat, an American. Portnoy is his name, Port-noy.

HE TRIES SPELLING IT OUT IN FRENCH TO THE ARAB. THE
ARAB NODS.

ARAB: Port-noy.

BILLY: Very good. His number, numéro, is Etoile,
got that, Etoile 3466, 3-4-6-6. Got that? Tell him
Billy Ade, that's me, c'est moi, is in jail. To
help, compris?, to help me.

THE JAILER HAS OPENED THE DOOR, BECKONS FOR THE
ARAB.

BILLY: Are you sure you understand? Port-noy.
Lawyer, Etoile 3466. Me. Billy Ade. Jail. Please.

THE ARAB SMILES, TOUCHES HIS FOREHEAD, LIPS,
CHEST. BILLY, IN OVERWHELMING GRATITUDE, CLUMSILY
DOES THE SAME. THE DOOR CLANGS SHUT.

SQUARE: Will he do it?

BILLY: Why should he, nobody does anything for him,
do they?

HOODLUM: They buy . . . his . . . peanuts.

BILLY:

(TO SQUARE)

I worked for Portnoy when I first got here. Nice
guy, I used to handle money for him all the time,
he ought to know I wouldn't be fooling around with
bedsheets.

(SHAKING SQUARE)

He would, wouldn't he?

SQUARE: Relax, Billy Boy. I don't think that Ay-rab
understood a word you said.

THIS CAMERA HOLDS ON A CLOSE-UP OF BILLY'S LARGE FACE.

SQUARE'S VOICE: Buck up, Billy Boy. What are you going to do when you get out?

NO ANSWER.

Are you going to finish up that novel?

NO ANSWER.

I mean what are you going to do when it's finished?

BILLY: I'm going to run.

SQUARE: What are you talking about?

BILLY: Run like crazy?

SQUARE: Where, man, where?

BILLY: Away from this place.

SQUARE: Come off it.

BILLY: Shut up.

SQUARE: Where will you go? Siberia?

HOODLUM:

(LAUGHING)

The Cameroons, where everyone is black.

BILLY: I said shut up!

SQUARE: Easy, Billy Boy.

BILLY: Don't put your hands on me.

(NEAR TEARS)

I've got to get out of here, I can't stand it!

(SOBBING)

I don't have anywhere to run.

HOODLUM: American boy, listen to me. My mother was poor and my father was somewhere else, and I ran away and I am here, am I not black? I went back when I was your age but my mother was gone and there was no back to go to, and so I am here. When a policeman sees me, I do nothing, I am in jail, am I not black? Go home, boy, go home!

BILLY: This isn't America!

HOODLUM: In America they have Negroes and thieves, and here we have Arabs and thieves, there is always someone and thieves, go home!

SQUARE: Billy Boy, beat it down, Paris is a great town and we'll be out of here free as a bird. . . .

HOODLUM: Go home!

BILLY: Leave me alone!

HE IS CROUCHED IN THE CORNER.

HOODLUM: Why are you crying?

BILLY: Paris . . .

(HE SNIFFLES)

. . . is a beautiful . . . city. . . .

HOODLUM: Is that a reason to cry?

BILLY: Paris is a beautiful city but it is not my home.

A FACE APPEARS AT THE JUDAS HOLE. THE DOOR OPENS. IT IS THE JAILER. HE POINTS TO BILLY, WHO SNIFFS BACK HIS TEARS.

JAILER: You!

SQUARE GETS SET TO GO WITH HIM.

No! This one. You stay here.

THE CAMERA HOLDS ON SQUARE'S FRIGHTENED FACE. DISSOLVE TO THE JAILER AND BILLY ENTERING A ROOM. MAURICE PORTNOY, THE LAWYER, GREETS BILLY.

MAURICE: Billy Ade, I wouldn't believe my ears when I heard—

BILLY:

WIPING BACK HIS TEARS.

Maurice! The Arab?

MAURICE: I gave him a hundred francs, just in case what he said was true.

BILLY HUGS MAURICE, HIS EYES BRIMMING.

BILLY: Maurice, I was never so glad, never.

MAURICE: Tell me what happened.

AS THEY HUDDLE AND WHISPER, THE CAMERA STUDIES THE PASSIVE FACE OF THE JAILER, WHO IS PLAYING WITH HIS EAR.

MAURICE: You've got nothing to worry about.

BILLY: I can come with you?

MAURICE: It's not easy, I'll put in a couple of quick calls, we'll have to get you before a judge, which would be, let's see, day after tomorrow, two more days, how's that?

BILLY: Maurice, it's been six days already, has my hair turned white?

MAURICE: I wish I had known sooner.

HE SLIPS BILLY A PACK OF CIGARETTES WHILE EMBRAC-
ING HIM.

BILLY: Thanks.

MAURICE: Shhh. Good-bye.

AS SOON AS MAURICE IS GONE, THE JAILER MOTIONS
BILLY TO HAND OVER THE CIGARETTES. THE JAILER
SMILES. AS HE LEADS BILLY OFF, WE HEAR. . .

BILLY'S VOICE: A night and a day and a night and it
was the day after tomorrow.

SQUARE: We're free!

BILLY AND SQUARE ARE PUTTING THEIR BELTS ON AND
LACING THEIR SHOES HURRIEDLY.

BILLY: As a bird!

BILLY FINISHES FIRST. HE'S OFF.

SQUARE: Man, where you rushing?

BILLY:

(ON THE FLY)

I'll see you later.

SQUARE: Wait a minute!

BILLY: Can't. I've made up my mind.

DISSOLVE FROM THE COURTROOM TO FILM CLIPS OF PARIS—
THE CITY, THE RUSHING TRAFFIC, ONE OR TWO OF THE FA-
MILIAR LANDSCAPES, WHIRLING, TURNING, WE HEAR THE
SOUND OF A HEART RACING AS BILLY RUNS, RUNS, RUNS TO
THE CAFE WHERE HE HAD MET SIDDY EIGHT DAYS AGO. HE
STOPS BEFORE THE EMPTY TABLES. THEN, AS HE STARES,
FROM BEHIND HIM, A VOICE.

SIDDY'S VOICE: Looking for someone?

BILLY WHIRLS.

BILLY: Siddy!

SIDDY: Oh I couldn't leave, I couldn't leave. I knew
something had happened, that you wouldn't just *not*
come back, I knew you'd find your way back, but it
took so long, so long.

THEY ARE IN EACH OTHER'S ARMS.

BILLY: Siddy, listen, I'm coming with you. I'm going
to Switzerland.

SIDDY: It's a free country.

BILLY: You don't know the half of it!

SIDDY: And after Switzerland, will you come back to
New York, I'd love to do a portrait of you . . . in
New York.

BILLY: What will your father say?

SIDDY: He'll say, "Crazy girl, what do you want to do <u>that</u> for?"

THEY LAUGH.

SIDDY: And I'll tell him, oh will I tell him!

BILLY: Siddy, look at me.

SIDDY: Yes?

BILLY: I'm going back home.

SIDDY: For me?

BILLY: For me, too. Running away didn't solve anything.

SIDDY: No.

BILLY: It just helped me find you.

SIDDY: Just?

BILLY: And myself.

BACKGROUND MUSIC AND TRAFFIC NOISES MOUNT TO A CLIMAX AS SIDDY AND BILLY, ARM IN ARM, WALK OFF INTO THE PARIS STREETS.

About the Authors

For thirty-six years SOL STEIN edited and published some of the most successful writers of the century, including James Baldwin, David Frost, Jack Higgins, Elia Kazan, Dylan Thomas, Lionel Trilling, and three heads of state. He is himself a prize-winning playwright produced on Broadway, an anthologized poet, and the author of nine novels plus nonfiction books, screenplays, and TV dramas. Stein has been interviewed on numerous national TV shows.

JAMES BALDWIN was born on August 2, 1924, and educated in New York. His first novel, *Go Tell It on the Mountain,* published in 1953, was immediately recognized as establishing a profound and permanent new voice in American letters. The legendary *Notes of a Native Son* was published in 1955. He continued to write fiction, poetry, and plays for the rest of his career. Baldwin was made a commander of the French Legion of Honor in June 1986. Among the other awards he received are a Eugene F. Saxon Memorial Trust Award, a Rosenwald fellowship, a Guggenheim fellowship, a Partisan Review fellowship, and a Ford Foundation grant. James Baldwin died at his home in St.-Paul-de-Vence in France on December 1, 1987.

ABOUT THE TYPE

This book was set in Sabon, a typeface designed by the well-known German typographer Jan Tschichold (1902–74). Sabon's design is based upon the original letter forms of Claude Garamond and was created specifically to be used for three sources: foundry type for hand composition, Linotype, and Monotype. Tschichold named his typeface for the famous Frankfurt typefounder Jacques Sabon, who died in 1580.